"What people ar

Ms. Plunkett's experiences are evidence that change and learning occur at the school level. Her journey, sprinkled with her English major's analogies and elder's wisdom, illustrates the incomparable responsibility of the school principal. She describes in-the-moment decisions and intentional actions of principled leadership. Her "walk the walk" stories pique the most seasoned educators' "how?" and "why?" curiosity of each situation. Her anecdotes exemplify leadership where decisions are genuinely made in the best interest of the students, not convenience or placating adults. If you ever attended school (insert smiley face) or served as an educator, you will experience Ms. Plunkett's principal's presence and stories of timeless relevance.

– Jere Hochman, Ed.D
Former Superintendent

The authentic storytelling in this book is infused with compelling wisdom and purpose. It truly inspires leading with empathy and guiding a school leader's work through the lens of what is best for students. This easy read will move you to not only think differently, but motivate you to move forward in an insightful and thoughtful way. Whether you work in or with a school, have kids in school, or went to school, you will not only enjoy *Lessons That Endure* but appreciate the gentle reminders to lead as you want to be led!

– Douglas P. Thaman, Ed.D
Executive Director
Missouri Charter Public School Association

The eye-popping tales of a high school principal make *Lessons That Endure* captivating to read. Ms. Plunkett deftly weaves the thinking of distinguished educators into the narrative for insight and reflection and punctuates her message with quotes from a varied and entertaining ensemble of writers, statesmen, and musicians. From Thomas Sergiovanni to Jimmy Buffett, the wisdom of their words adds clarity to the moment. Funny, tender, even shocking, her stories are true, which means they can be as heartbreaking as they are inspiring. This is a book for every administrator, teacher, and parent, for that matter, to read.

– Nan R. Johnson
Author, *The Open Road* by M.M. Holaday

Lessons That Endure is a must-read for all school leaders! While the specific situations might vary by school or age of students, the lessons truly are ones that endure and are meaningful for leaders of any school community. I was incredibly fortunate to serve as an assistant principal where Beth was principal. She inspired us all daily and taught me what it means to be a servant leader. Every school leader will benefit from reading about her thoughtful approach to creating a caring school community, where caring about others is modeled by the leader every day and in every situation she faces.

– Jenny Marquart, Ed.D
Retired Principal, Parkway North High School
Parkway School District

LESSONS
THAT
ENDURE

REFLECTIONS OF A
HIGH SCHOOL PRINCIPAL

BETH PLUNKETT

Lessons That Endure
Reflections of a High School Principal
Beth Plunkett
Plunkett Page

Published by Plunkett Page, Fresno, California

Editor: Karen Tucker, CommaQueenEditing.com

Cover and Interior design: Davis Creative, CreativePublishingPartners.com

Back cover photo: Alexandra Pacheco Garcia

Library of Congress Cataloging-in-Publication Data

Library of Congress Control Number: 2022905196

Beth Plunkett

Lessons That Endure: Reflections of a High School Principal

ISBN: 979-8-9855444-0-4 (paperback)
      979-8-9855444-1-1 (hardback)

BISAC Subject headings:

1. EDU001020 EDUCATION / Administration / Elementary &
    Secondary 2. EDU032000 EDUCATION / Leadership
    3. EDU040000 EDUCATION /Philosophy, Theory & Social Aspects

2022

ATTENTION CORPORATIONS, UNIVERSITIES, COLLEGES AND PROFESSIONAL ORGANIZATIONS: Quantity discounts are available on bulk purchases of this book for educational, gift purposes, or as premiums for increasing magazine subscriptions or renewals. Special books or book excerpts can also be created to fit specific needs. For information, please contact Plunkett Page, mebplunkett@gmail.com.

*In every conceivable manner,
the family is link to our past,
bridge to our future.*

– Alex Haley

*To the three who call me Mom—
Kevin, Jeffrey, Matthew*

Table of Contents

Introduction

The essential conditions of everything
you do must be choice, love, passion.

– Nadia Boulanger

On the July night in 1992 that the Parkway School District appointed me a first-time principal, my niece called. Johanna was nine years old and in the third grade at the time. We were still using phones that were wired to a wall back then, so I picked up on the fourth ring.

Johanna dismissed my greeting and brusquely muttered, "Daddy just told me that you're going to be the principal of a school."

I was confused by her accusatory tone but confirmed her father's intel. There was a long pause. "Johanna," I questioned, "what's going on? What's the matter?"

"Well, Aunt Beth," Johanna sighed, "I just can't like you anymore. Nobody likes a principal."

I was bewildered. I assumed that Johanna would be proud of me; I was counting on her to be. Whatever experiences in her brief career as a student had shaped Johanna's opinion, I soon discovered that she was hardly alone in holding it.

One Saturday afternoon, after only six months on the job, I was in the grocery store when I heard a teenage voice call my name. I turned, and seeing one of my students, I called out cheerily, "Tommy! How great to see you!"

As I zigzagged through the produce aisle to speak with Tommy, I heard his father rebuke him, saying, "How does she know your name? What have you done?" For many, going to the principal's office was akin to going to war or to hell…or worse.

There was—and sadly, still is—an old-school theorem that predicts if a school administrator knows who you are, you've been in some kind of trouble.

My story documents the journey of my years as a principal. I hope it serves to help others who might aspire to the same position to see the amazing joy the role can hold, as well as the mind-bending responsibilities it brings. I have chosen to use narratives to reveal the lessons I learned on the job. I culled the stories from memory, of course, but also from a dozen journals I kept through the years, several binders of newsletters and memos that I had sent to the community (many from pre-email days), and, the sweetest of sources, conversations with colleagues and former students. As I assembled stories and ideas, I was struck by the pivotal influence my father, my chaotic childhood, and my children had on the leader I became.

From my father, I absorbed the importance of predictability; from the path of my childhood, the salience of process in human interaction; and, from raising my boys, the role of nonnegotiables in setting goals.

Mother died of a cerebral aneurism a week before my fourth birthday. Burdened with unthinkable grief, Dad drove us that night from the hospital in which Mom died to his mother's home in West Philadelphia. We never returned to our New Jersey home, and Dad never spoke of Mom until we were young adults and confident enough to ask. In the face of the loss of his young wife (Mom was twenty-nine when she died) and despite his chosen method to grieve, Dad remained a dependable and positive influence in our lives. From him I learned that reliably "showing up" for those you love creates an immutable bond of trust. My physical and emotional presence among those I served as principal became a salient aspect of my leadership style.

My brother, sister, and I were, admittedly, spoiled rotten by Dad's mother, Grandma Brecker, and the rest of the family. To compensate for Mom's loss, they withdrew all rules; we were lawless—but well-loved—toddlers. Consequently, when Dad remarried ten years later, and our stepmother brought reasonable expectations for our behavior (e.g., an established time to go to bed—really?), we were resentful. And we sure as hell resisted.

At the time of Dad's remarriage, Jim, Chris, and I were old enough to have been brought into any discussion about changes in daily routines. Some thirty-five years later, as I immersed myself in the complex world of school leadership, the significance of process in times of change was paramount. Including key players in the discussion and planning process does not always result in a universally acceptable plan, but it almost always allows buy-in. After eighteen years as a school leader, I know unequivocally that a principal who holds heartfelt and genuine respect for the people she serves has unquantified power to effect change, especially when the process itself is valued foremost.

In undergraduate psychology class, we learned about the Model of Concentric Circles. At the center of the model are the core values that an individual or a group of people such as a family or a school hold most dear. These are the nonnegotiables. As one moves out from the center, the circles expand to chronicle and prioritize the values held sacred by the entity. While I am 100 percent certain I did not pull out the aged notebook from that psych class, my parenting efforts were intuitively influenced by that model. I was really OK with my kids' wardrobe choices that paired floral shirts with plaid shorts. I was not OK if they treated their brothers or anybody else rudely. Kindness, honesty, and respect were the nonnegotiables in our house.

The author with her three sons: Kevin, Jeffrey, and Matthew

These lessons pulled through into my professional career. I didn't care how teachers assigned kids to seats in class—or even if they assigned seats at all—but I insisted that each child in every classroom at Fern Ridge High School and at Parkway West High felt welcomed, respected, and important to the learning that would take place.

The unpublished, working title of my tale was *You Can't Make This Shit Up*; trust me, I really couldn't. Just as witnesses to the same crime might report different versions of the facts, so, too, my account of events might differ from others who experienced them with me. But this is my story.

I think the most productive and effective people are those who are truly happy in their work. I was. Nadia Boulanger, a French essayist, captured the essence of that symbiosis for me: "The essential conditions of everything you do must be choice, love, passion." Choice. Love. Passion. I was all in.

Chapter 1 – The Demon of Discretionary Authority

Things which matter most must never be at the mercy of things which matter least.

– Johann Wolfgang von Goethe

My father was an amazing storyteller. I have nine siblings, and anytime a critical mass of us were around a table, we could count on Dad to entertain with a story. Whether the tales were true, as he alleged, is uncertain; they were, for sure, always laced with moral observations.

The author, second from the right, with her father, stepmother, and siblings at the wedding of sister Ann to Mark Miller

One Thanksgiving, just after we had said grace, Dad warned us that, because we were Breckers, we should always be polite and classy…or else. The glint in his eye cued us that we were about to hear a good one. And so began what Dad called "The Parrot's Tale." It went like this:

A young man named John received a parrot as a gift. The parrot had a bad attitude and an even worse vocabulary. Every word out of the bird's mouth was rude, obnoxious, and profane. John tried to change the bird's attitude by consistently saying only polite words, playing soft music, and anything else he could think of that could clean up the bird's language.

Finally, John was fed up, and he yelled at the bird. The parrot yelled back. John shook the parrot, and the parrot got angrier and even ruder. In desperation, John threw up his hands, grabbed the bird, and shoved him into the freezer. For a few minutes, the parrot squawked and kicked and screamed. Then, suddenly, there was silence.

Fearing that he'd hurt the feathered beast, John quickly opened the door to the freezer. The parrot calmly stepped out onto John's outstretched arm and said, "I believe I may have offended you with my rude language and actions. I am sincerely remorseful for my inappropriate transgressions, and I fully intend to do everything I can to correct my unforgiveable behavior."

John was stunned. As he was about to ask the parrot what had caused such a dramatic shift in attitude, the bird continued, "May I ask what the turkey did?"

I entered the field of education just after my college graduation in 1970, and, until I retired in 2010, a sign hung behind my desk that helped me to keep the parrot's tale in mind. A reminder of one reason we should treat people respectfully, regardless of the situation, the sign bore this wry observation:

"Veterinarian or taxidermist: either way,

you get your dog back."

Many times, despite all our proactive work, and in the face of deliberately placed interventions, kids and adults do stupid things. Sometimes, they even do bad things. Regardless of the heinousness of an individual's actions or words, I resolved always to treat the "sinner" with dignity. A principal's decision-making is sometimes mandated by state or federal law, sometimes dictated by district policy, and sometimes merely rooted in old-fashioned common sense. But sometimes a sticky wicket called "principal's discretion" muddies the water.

One morning during my first year as a Parkway West Longhorn, I heard a call on my walkie-talkie to come to the senior locker bay. During passing periods, the senior locker bay was one of the most congested areas in our building. Located on the third floor, the area was home to 250 student lockers and marked the intersection of the English and social studies departments. When the bell rang at the end of a class, no fewer than forty classrooms of twenty-plus students each emptied into this sector. It was loud, it was crowded, and on this morning, it was the scene of a bloody fight.

As I hurried toward the locker bay, I observed an agitated crowd gathered around Christopher, one of our most popular senior men. Christopher was holding his face, seriously swearing, and bleeding profusely. I called for the nurse and dispersed the onlookers and sympathizers to their next classes. Christopher was in considerable pain, and to my somewhat practiced eye (I have nine siblings, three sons, and, at that point, twenty-two years as a high school teacher), his nose appeared to be broken.

After the school nurse had cleaned up Christopher's face, applied an ice pack, and confirmed the likelihood of a broken proboscis, the young man told me what had happened. For a very long time, by his own admission, Christopher had been hurling insults and degrading comments at Sam Wagner whenever he saw him in the halls. On this particular day, for no reason Christopher could summon, Sam freaked out when Christopher called him a *crippled gimp.*

"I've called him that a hundred times," Chris offered. "Why did he wig out this time?"

Every part of me was in disbelief. How could Sam Wagner have done this? He was one of the kindest, gentlest souls I knew... and being so made him an easy target for a bully like Christopher.

Sam had suffered a stroke as a middle school child. He made a full recovery cognitively but was left with a speech impediment and the partial paralysis of his left side. When I sought him out later to hear his version of events, Sam was crestfallen and scared. He had never acted out in school before and wanted only to know if Christopher was OK.

"I just flipped out," he said. "I had listened to him and his friends taunt me and make fun of me as long as I could. I just wanted him to stop."

Sam's was a pattern of behavior that I had seen play out too many times before. Rather than referring an issue to an appropriate authority, the victim chooses to take matters into his own hands. In so doing, the victim becomes a guilty person. But how guilty was he, given the persistent, baleful harangues of his verbal aggressor? In truth, there were two aggressors that day, and I found myself in the throes of a moral dilemma as to how to proceed. Clearly both young men had acted badly, but was one offense more egregious than the other? The family whose son's nose was broken believed so; I was unsure. On a guttural level, I knew that persistent bullying taunts have a visceral pain of their own. And there were other external factors at play—factors that, in retrospect, I had no business considering.

I was in my first year as head principal at West High. Every major decision was a test: a test of my toughness and a test of my ability to read the school culture and respond accordingly. This had been a highly visible encounter between two well-known students. Although years later I would understand the fallacy in my thinking, on that day I believed I needed to respond in a way that sent this message: everything's under control. The faculty was watching, and

I grabbed the heavy hammer. I suspended Sam Wagner for ten days and Christopher for three. I chose to assign consequences without regard to the history of taunting and abuse that had characterized Chris's behavior and that had precipitated Sam's.

In his column *The Ethicist*, Randy Cohen observes, "Sometimes ethics delineates only what is acceptable, not what is admirable." The incident between the boys should have been a forum to teach all involved what I knew in my heart: emotional violence is as painful and as wrong as physical violence. In the rush to "prove myself" to the faculty, I lacked the certitude—and the courage—in that moment to mete out more equitable consequences. Both families accepted my decisions with little pushback, and I was reminded of the power and the influence of the lead dog. Yet I resolved never to be distracted again by unrelated concerns. The job should never be as much about the authority you have to punish as it is about the opportunity to teach. Therein lie both the liberties and the limitations of discretionary authority: What we *can* do and what we *ought* to do are two separate things. In retrospect, I failed both boys. District policy called for me to respond to the misbehavior on both sides of the locker bay that day, and I did that. It was my discretionary decision-making that was flawed. A few years later, I did a better job with Aaron.

Just after the lunch period ended on a warm April afternoon, one of my juniors slouched into my office mumbling, "Plunkett, you're gonna be mad."

"Hi, Aaron," I smiled at the young man I knew well and then asked innocently, "What on earth could you ever do to make me mad?"

"Oh, besides smoking on campus and being sent to ISS, like, every other week?" was his smug response.

Our ISS was an in-school suspension room and program where we assigned kids for what we referred to as "crimes that hurt only themselves." Skipping class was the second most popular ticket to ISS; smoking on campus was number one. Aaron's self-proclaimed admission was pretty much on target, but I was more alarmed that he smoked a fair amount of marijuana as well. At that time, marijuana was illegal to possess or use. The odor his clothes emitted often betrayed his after-school habit, but I truly believed he stuck to Marlboros on campus.

Most high schools (and a good many middle schools, I fear) have a percentage of kids for whom smoking marijuana—AKA reefer, dope, nickel bags—was a well-entrenched habit. I referred to students who fell into this group as *fringe kids*. Their academic performance and, often, their social acumen were compromised by their use of drugs, and so, in my vernacular, that put them on the fringe of their true potential. I rejected the use of more pejorative terms like *stoner, burnout,* or *pothead* because they implied a permanent relegation to that status. I preferred to believe that with guidance and maturity—and, perhaps, with enough unwanted consequences—they could and would make a change. On this particular spring day, however, Aaron was apparently not yet there.

Aaron told me that after he ate lunch earlier, he had walked to a notoriously famous stairwell at the back of our four-story schoolhouse. The stairwell exited to a wooded area of campus frequented by nefarious smokers of all sorts of stuff. Since the late nineties, all campus doors were set to lock from the outside automatically. This was not Aaron's first rodeo. So, as he approached the door to go outside for a smoke, he removed his wallet and placed it in the doorjamb to ensure his safe reentry to the building. Alas, as Aaron related to me, when he returned after his indulgence, the wallet was gone and the door was securely locked. With much chagrin and very little eye contact, Aaron acknowledged that ISS would be once again in his near future, but he had just cashed his paycheck, and he needed that money badly. I didn't ask for what.

In the moment of reporting, victims don't need to be chastised for their actions that allowed an opportunity for a crime to occur. Aaron knew quite well that if he hadn't decided to go outside to smoke, his wallet—and his cash—would still be in his pants. Instead of belaboring the obvious, I told him that I would do everything I could to find out who had taken his wallet. "We'll deal with the smoking on campus later," I told him, as I sent him back to class.

In the post-Columbine years of the late nineties, our school district had also installed ubiquitous security cameras. Every entrance to the building was surveilled, every hall, every stairwell. The district had a team of security officers who monitored the cameras remotely. On campus, ours was a passive surveillance. We accessed the cameras and their taped recordings only when necessary. In this case, it was necessary. Aaron had not seen anyone in the area prior to propping the door. We had no choice but to view the tapes from that stairwell and to see what we could see. And, oh brother, what we saw.

I never cared to learn how to manipulate the machines that stored the videotapes, so I asked Jack Ryan, the building manager, to help me locate the film from the appropriate time frame. As Jack scrolled to the window of time in question, I saw a junior student whom (until then) I knew only by face. The film showed the young man, whom events would reveal as Adrian, bounding down the stairs, looking cautiously around. We watched as he spotted the wallet in the door, removed it, and pocketed it. Then he called up the stairs, "It's all clear, Gina, come on down."

Gina and Adrian then proceeded to lie down in the stairwell and immediately, under the camera's unflinching eye, have sex. I certainly then knew more than Adrian's face. I called him by his full name when I went to his sixth-hour class and told him that we needed to discuss something that had happened at lunch. He compliantly followed me into the hall as we walked to my office.

"Oh," teenage lover boy said as he removed the purloined wallet from his pocket, "I meant to bring this to you. I found it during lunch." Indeed.

A few minutes later, seated in my conference room along with his grade-level principal, I told Adrian I suspected he might have had yet another adventure at lunch. He seemed bewildered, and so I switched gears.

"Do you remember the class meetings we hold at the start of each semester?" I asked.

"Yeah," he said with a laugh, "you say the same things over and over each time."

"How about surveillance cameras?" I questioned gently. "Do you remember me saying anything about where the cameras are positioned around the school?"

With an unforgettable, fused look of comprehension and utter embarrassment, Adrian dropped his head to the table with an expletive that suited the event in question. To his mumbled inquiry, I assured him that I had indeed watched the tape.

Phone calls to both participants' families followed to explain why suspensions from school would be necessary, but it was my follow-up conversation with Aaron that prompts me to tell this story.

When I called him to my office and returned his wallet with all the cash still inside, Aaron was nonplussed. "Damn," he said, "you're good. Thanks. I guess I'm going to ISS tomorrow, huh?"

I knew I had an opportunity, a vulnerable moment in Aaron's life, to teach the bigger lesson of the day's events. I'm not sure Aaron even believed I'd make an effort to find something stolen from someone *like him*. He was focused on the fact that he became a victim because he had chosen to be a rule breaker and assumed he'd be punished.

School leaders ought to have reasonable latitude in enforcing district expectations for behavior. The arbitrary one-size-fits-all model of the Procrustean bed is well-documented from Greek myth. According to legend, Procrustes was a villainous innkeeper who made a habit of fitting his guests to the only bed he owned by lopping off their legs if they were too tall or torturously stretching them if too short. Typically, American schools' consequences are less severe, but the lesson still holds. This was a repeated infraction for Aaron; I was well within my rights to remove him from his classes.

The Australian politician Anna Bligh once commented, "Leadership is what you see when the rule book runs out." I chose an alternate option with Aaron.

I knew he was deeply indebted to me for following through, finding the thief, and returning his possessions to him. I decided to play those cards and ask for a favor in return: I would waive the "mandatory" ISS sentence if he would promise to never smoke on campus again. He seemed more eager for the deal than I thought he might be and accepted quickly. I promised to support him (I always kept hard candy, chocolate, and gum around to help kids and teachers cope with stress), and I also warned Aaron that if he broke his end of the deal, the consequences would be more significant. I was rewarded with Aaron's most beautiful smile, a nod, and a quick exit from my office. For many teenagers, trusting adults—especially principal-type adults—can be a problem, but for those with substance issues, it's a big obstacle. I'm pretty sure Aaron hightailed it that day thinking I might change my mind.

Flash forward to Aaron's graduation day fourteen months later. We graduated about 325 young adults each year, and the ceremony was held in a cavernous facility owned by the St. Louis County Parks. The night of Aaron's graduation, he called me over to a side hallway where he was adjusting his academic cap and gown. He would never have spoken to me in front of the "cool" kids in his class: the athletes, the summa cum laudes, or even the techies. Each of them had a niche during their high school years. Aaron did too, of course, but the fringe kids didn't have a school sponsor.

Aaron asked me if I remembered the deal we had made during his junior year. When I assured him that I did, he nodded and, looking me squarely in the eye, admitted, "I broke my word once, very soon after that wallet deal. Although I didn't get caught, I felt so guilty because you had given me a second chance…and because you trusted me. I wish I could tell you that I've quit smoking, but that would be a lie. But I will tell you that I never smoked again on campus. So, thanks. Thanks for standing up for me when I never believed anyone at this school cared." I never needed prompts to start my tears on graduation night, but Aaron's words dissolved me.

In the spot-on, absolutely accurate words of the historian Henry Adams, "A teacher affects eternity; he can never tell where his influence stops." Principals are teachers first—and always. We must never use our authority to marginalize kids, even when— or *especially* when—their behaviors or attitudes run counter to a school's central beliefs. I am deeply grateful for Aaron's courage and maturity in speaking with me as he did on his graduation night. He reminded me that, as educators, we can teach our students all the math, science, and humanities their heads can hold, but if we fail to challenge them to be people of character and integrity, we have failed them.

It is an easy task to recognize the outstanding academic achievement of our top echelon of students, and it is imperative that we do. The rule-breaking low achievers can wear us out, to be sure. But to quit on them, I believe, is to betray the fundamental responsibility entrusted to us as school leaders. It was the legendary football coach Vince Lombardi who opined, "Fatigue makes cowards of us all." Effective school leadership has no room for cowards. Embrace the kids on the fringe; they may not maximize their learning opportunities during their years of high school, but if they emerge from our stewardship as stronger, more self-aware individuals because of our unconditional support, they will find their niche in this world. I believe Aaron did.

In her inspired book, *The Gifts of Imperfection*, Brené Brown puts a more sophisticated spin on the veterinarian or taxidermist adage. She wrote, "It's hard for us to understand that we can be compassionate and accepting while we hold people accountable for their behaviors." One year, when a student with whom I had a close relationship behaved very badly, Brown's observation was tested.

Depending on the sport, our school competed in various conferences and districts as defined by Missouri's governing board for high school athletics and activities, MSHSAA. One winter afternoon, our boys' swim team traveled to a prestigious private school in a tony St. Louis suburb. A natural rivalry occurred among all the public and private high schools in our region, but between West High and the private sector, there was an added edge.

Living in an upper middle-class neighborhood, a high percentage of the families I served could well afford to send their kids to the exclusive private academies, but they chose the public system instead. These decisions were based, proudly, on our excellent reputation as a college preparatory school. We sent our graduates to the best schools in the country—and we were "free." Many of our students were also second-generation Longhorns. Tradition was strong; alumni were loyal.

On this particular day, I did not attend the swim meet, but I met the school bus as it returned to campus about 6:30 that night. To my horror, the boys emerged from the bus chanting our fight song, many wearing the host school's football helmets and jerseys. I was outraged.

Stepping coatless out into the cold January night, I thundered, "Stop right there. All of you, back on the bus. Now."

I tend to be an even-tempered person. I understand the impact of a principal's mood and attitude on the overall climate of a building, and my constituencies would describe me, I think, as a predictably fair, kind, and well-spoken administrator. But not that night. I could summon none of Brené Brown's "compassionate and accepting" words. I was livid.

Certain that my face was crimson with rage, I stood next to the embarrassed bus driver, who only wanted to get out of his seat and go home, and said to the suddenly silent swim team, "What on God's earth have you done?"

No one made eye contact or spoke. I searched their faces, hoping to burn my indignation into their souls. Then I saw the team captain. "Steven," I said, "stand up."

Steven Smith was a seventeen-year-old senior with whom I had had a strong, personal relationship throughout his four years at school. He rarely missed an opportunity to poke his head into my office when passing to simply call, "Hey, Ms. P. How ya doing?" That night, you'd have thought we were strangers.

In a steely voice, I said, "Steven, as captain of this team, I need an explanation as to why you and your teammates are sitting in front of me wearing equipment and clothing that belongs to another school."

I thought he might cry, and I did nothing to ease his discomfort. Instead, I called on my radio for the other administrator in the building to meet me at the bus. And then, with deliberate calm, clear enunciation, and riveting eye contact with the team, I asked my colleague to call the police to meet the bus as well.

It was a very long night; we called each swimmer's parents and asked them to come to campus. Not everyone on the team had stolen from the host school, but I wanted every family to be aware of the situation firsthand. In education, we probably overuse the phrase "a teachable moment," but if there ever was one, this was it.

There were two conversation strands: one with the boys who had stolen, in some cases, hundreds of dollars of equipment (football helmets aren't cheap); and the other with those who witnessed the thefts and did nothing to stop the crimes. Common elements in both conversations, however, were the privilege of representing our school as an athlete and the importance of personal integrity. Education is a moral endeavor. On that evening, I was never more cognizant of the fact that not everyone was raised by my father.

There were other complicating circumstances. Steven, the swim team captain, and two others had already qualified for the state meet that was to be held the following week. A suspension from school—and clearly, stealing was a suspendible offense— would eliminate them from participation. That was MSHSAA's rule. And I knew it well.

Although I knew that my decision would deprive the affected athletes of a once-in-a-lifetime experience, I never hesitated to suspend them. I explained to each family that I hoped the lessons learned from this event would prepare them for other—argu- ably more significant—moments of glory. Most parents agreed. Steven's did not.

It was well after midnight when I got home that night, exhausted and truly hurting for the boys, their families, and for our school's reputation. In truth, I was also embarrassed as hell. I knew how these things worked. For sure, I had a difficult phone call to make the next morning to the head of the school from which my kids had stolen. We had to return the pilfered goods, and since a police report was filed, there was a strong possibility that the media would have a field day. My heart was adequately aching already when, at 7:30 the next morning, Steven and his father showed up, unannounced, in my office.

When they arrived, I was not in the office area. Our students began filling the halls at seven each morning, and I was always out and about, checking in on them as well as the teachers and staff. Some educational writers call this leadership style MBWA—Management by Walking Around. I preferred to think of it as leading from within.

My insightful secretary, Lauren, was always able to read an emerging situation well. I had not had a chance to fill her in on the events of the night before, but she quickly surmised that I should see this father and his son immediately, despite the lack of an appointment. When Lauren contacted me on the walkie, I returned to the office right away.

It would be an understatement to say the conversation got a jump start. Steven's father arrived in a rage, and things disintegrated from there. He spoke of his son's outstanding academic career during high school. I agreed; Steven was one of our top scholars. He spoke of his son's spotless discipline record. I assured Dad that he was not wrong. Then he asked me if none of this counted. And therein was the coaching crucible.

I told Mr. Smith—and Steven—that Steven's academic achievements, athletic accomplishments, and good behavior should not be discredited or forgotten. However, none of these positives could erase this serious indiscretion nor the need for inherent consequences. The father listened carefully, but his response rattled my core.

Mr. Smith asked me if I had seen his son steal anything from the school the previous night. I assured him that I had not been in the boys' locker room and did not personally witness the thefts.

"How then," the father challenged, "do you know that Steven actually took anything himself?"

"Well, sir," I responded, "Steven told me he did."

Implausibly, Steven's father challenged, "Ask him again."

I was flabbergasted. I stood and ended the meeting by saying, "I will not do that, sir. I will not ask your son to compromise his integrity. The suspension stands. If you would like to speak to my supervisor, my secretary can give you pertinent information."

The bottom line: Steven was suspended, eliminated from the state meet, and never swam for our school again. Mr. Smith exhausted every appeal available to him without recourse, and he never forgave me. But I believe Steven understood. To honor his otherwise outstanding citizenship and scholarship, I exercised one of the discretionary options I had and allowed him to participate in graduation. As he accepted his diploma, Steven's nod and demurred smile verified that my message had been received. He had screwed up big time, but, if this was the worst thing he ever did, he was going to be OK.

By refusing to back down from my decision to suspend Steven, I opened myself, and our school, to highly visible and negative attention. The Smiths' appeals were to the superintendent, the board of education, and, ultimately, to MSHSAA itself. In each case, I needed to appear in person to explain and defend my decision. Had I acquiesced to Mr. Smith's demand and asked his son if he had stolen from the locker room that night, it is likely, given the familial pressure, that Steven would have denied any wrongdoing. With regard to a responsibility to suspend, I'd have been off the hook, and Steven would have represented us at the state meet. Lacking any other evidence, trusting a student's statement of fact is a defensible option for a principal in most circumstances. But, in the words of the German thinker Goethe, "Things which matter most must never be at the mercy of things which matter least."

As I defended my discretionary decision at various levels of appeals, my audience was much larger than I would have chosen, but then, my influence became broader as well. As a school leader, the courage to take a stand for the greater good should always trump expedience. We owe it to all whom we serve, and we owe it to ourselves as people of integrity.

Throughout my tenure as a head of school, countless other situations arose in which I had leeway to exercise discretionary authority. Responding to suspected child abuse or neglect, however, was never one.

The state of Missouri views educators as "mandated reporters." In that capacity, if we observe or suspect that a child has been abused, we must notify the Department of Social Services within twenty-four hours. To neglect that responsibility is a Class A misdemeanor. Over my eighteen years as a principal, I saw evidence of abuse too damn often. Frequently, we learned of the abuse from the victims themselves, but, more often, we were alerted to a concern by a staff member who knew the child well.

It goes without saying (I hope!) that teachers must develop relationships with their students in order to meet their cognitive needs. Only in a physically and emotionally safe classroom can children truly thrive, and no one can create that environment without knowing the needs of the people in the room. For whom will the novel about a parent's death be a trigger? For whom is last night's news about a shooting in a synagogue a blistering affront? And how will responses to these events present in the classroom? How will the teacher know? More importantly, how can the teacher anticipate these responses and plan for them?

A television commercial that aired a few years ago vividly demonstrated the impact of a compassionate and responsive teacher. A young Asian child is pictured in a tearful goodbye with his mother at a classroom door. It is clearly his first day at a new school. The teacher takes his hand and walks him into the room, standing with him in front of the class. "Girls and boys," the teacher says, "I'd like you to meet Chen."

As the little boy timorously raises his eyes, his new classmates stand and welcome him in his native language of Mandarin, calling, "Ni hao." A smile creeps across the young boy's face, and a tagline winds across the TV screen: "Anticipate."

When done well, the task of teaching young people merely begins with the established curriculum. My expectations were for all who interfaced with our students to care for them in a similarly vigilant manner, as the best teachers do.

The cafeteria staff, the custodial team, the secretarial pool, and the bus drivers must own the responsibility of and the rewards for establishing relationship with all whom they serve. After all, the bus drivers are often the first adults to see children after they have left their homes on any given morning. That makes them potential barometers of well-being. I needed the bus drivers to see the kids not merely as riders on their vehicles but as young people whom they were entrusted to transport safely to school. There's a subtle but extraordinarily important difference in those approaches. If a driver sensed that something was bothering a child, I needed to know. The same was true of any of the other adults in the building. More often than not, the change in attitude was nothing more than teenage angst over a love-gone-wrong or an argument with Mom over curfew. But we resolved together not to take that chance.

Over the years, we adopted an aphorism that summarized in quotable form what we believed to be essential about a successful school:

> Take care of yourself.
> Take care of each other.
> Take care of this place.

If a student arrived at school with bruising or wounds that appeared suspicious, we were duty bound by law to investigate, but we were mission bound to care. And there, in the caring, lay the moral quandary. A call to the state would initiate an immediate investigation. If the suspected abuse was occurring in the home, and this was most often the case, the child would not be allowed to return to that home until any threat of danger had been removed. We worried always that our making a report could ultimately make conditions worse for the young person. An adult who would intentionally hurt a child would not hesitate to exact revenge for being reported. Our calls to the state could initiate a worse cycle of violence...and we knew it. They are referred to as "hotline calls" for a reason. Yet there was no discretionary decision-making in these situations. We would make the call and then double down on our supports for the child. As head of school, I was always apprised when a staff member hotlined a student. On that, I insisted. I once had an assistant principal describe me as "overly involved." I'll own that; and in matters such as child abuse, I don't believe there's another way to be. A school leader must have the pulse of her school. At the other end of the spectrum of discretionary authority, however, is my memory of Carlos Garcia.

Carlos was a high-energy young man whose vibrant personality had a penchant for practical jokes. For this, he was infamous. In the spring of his senior year, Carlos decided he wanted to give the keynote address at graduation.

We had an audition process. All senior students could try out if they were in good standing, that is, if they had had no serious discipline infractions and if they were passing all of their classes. Each year we had about twenty-five students who tossed their hats into the ring for consideration. Each wrote and presented to a faculty panel a three-minute version of their proposed graduation remarks; I was always on that panel. The faculty then selected the top five speakers based on the message they chose and the confidence and poise with which they delivered it. Next, a senior class meeting was called, and the five selected speakers presented their speeches to the class, who voted and placed them in rank order. The top vote getter would win the coveted title of commencement speaker. Carlos's audition before the faculty panel was easily the best; he was witty, insightful, and as convincing as a politician with a stump speech. When he took the podium in front of his class, however, things changed.

Although students had been carefully coached to give the same speech in front of their peers as they had given before the faculty, Carlos broke rank. His delivery style was urbane and fluid, to be sure, but his content had changed. To the delight of some and the surprise and shock of many (most notably, me), Carlos bashed certain teachers by name, creating verbal caricatures of their peculiarities as he saw them. The trite but meaningful expression "if looks could kill" came quickly into play that afternoon in the theater. The teenage soul being what it is, Carlos was ranked first on a vast majority of ballots. And I had myself a serious dilemma. Process is important; we had told the seniors that any of the five speeches they would hear would be an appropriate choice—their choice—for graduation. I felt betrayed. In fact, however, the process had been betrayed.

I called Carlos at home that evening with the results of the balloting and asked him to come to my office the next morning with one of his parents. I also instructed him to be sure his parent knew why he or she had been asked to accompany him. To his credit, the young man was subdued and appropriate on the phone. He knew what he'd done was wrong. I just wasn't sure what I was going to do. The "easiest" solution would be to disqualify Carlos for not following the rules and award the speaker's honor to the second-highest vote getter. He'd abused the system, and he'd already had his moment in the limelight, albeit falsely attained.

Both Mom and Dad accompanied their son the next morning, and if there were awards given for outstanding parenting, they'd be hands-down winners. Undoubtedly at his parents' insistence, Carlos took the lead in the conversation.

"Mrs. Plunkett," he began, "I am really sorry. I have embarrassed my family and myself, and I have disappointed you beyond words."

"Thank you for the apology, Carlos," I responded. "It's all about trust, isn't it? You, the other speakers, and I had a covenant of sorts. And you betrayed the trust inherent in that agreement."

Mr. and Mrs. Garcia were native Mexicans, and they told me that both sets of Carlos's grandparents had already made airline reservations to attend graduation. It quickly became clear to me that the family feared Carlos would not be allowed to even participate in the ceremony, much less address the audience. I assured them that Carlos would be allowed to participate as a member of the graduating class; the unresolved question was whether he'd be on the stage as a speaker.

After a full hour of discussion, Carlos had impressed me with his understanding of his transgression and with his passionate desire to address his class the night of graduation. I saw the opportunity to teach, but I was wary of being duped again. I never made a habit of threatening students, so I promised Carlos that if he was given the privilege of speaking to his class, I would not hesitate to take the microphone from his hand at the slightest deviation from a preapproved script. Our graduation ceremony was held in a cavernous county-owned facility; upwards of 3,000 people would be in the audience—including his grandparents.

It was Carlos's father who sealed the deal for me when he said, "Mrs. Plunkett, you have my word. If Carlos changes his speech in any way, I myself will drag him from the stage. You won't have to do a thing."

Although I worried until the last word was out of his mouth, Carlos delivered an eloquent and respectful speech at graduation. He went on to become a high school teacher who, when I ran into him many years later, said to me, "I always, always give my students a second chance to make a better choice. Thank you, Mrs. Plunkett. You taught me that."

As we strive to lead, we must, of course, observe the law and, within our purview, enforce it. But if we stick to the "black and white," the predetermined options for leadership, we will miss all the power and possibility in the gray. Sometimes discretion is, indeed, the better part of valor.

Chapter 2 – The Chicken Run: Building a Cohesive School

It is not only for what we do that we are held responsible, but also for what we do not do.

– Molière

In the spring of 2003, I was talking with a student in the senior locker bay when it was time for the daily announcements. We both fell silent and listened to a member of our service society read a typical stream of club meetings, sporting events, and reminders. The final announcement, however, was unique. Three West High students were being recognized by Washington University in St. Louis as research scholars. After their names were read, Neil Feeney, the young man with whom I was seated, shook his head sadly and commented, "Do you know that I will graduate from high school next month and never, ever in all my years of school has my name been read over the public-address system? It's as though I was never here." I was touched by the poignancy and the significance of Neil's comment.

We were blessed to have many talented and intelligent young people at West High who frequently won awards and scholarships, league championships, marching band festivals and debate contests, to name but a smattering. Yet there were scores of other students walking our halls who, through choice or circumstances, might never receive public recognition. Neil was one. In a few weeks, I would sign his transcript, respectfully peppered with As and Bs, and I was sure he'd never even served an after-school detention. He had been a solid school citizen for four years. I assured Neil that day that his presence among us had made our school a better place. At the same time, I knew that his honesty had identified a significant need: nowhere in our school's scaffolding of recognitions and awards was there a place to acknowledge ordinary kids who get the job done without a lot of fanfare. I took the problem (because I saw it as one) to that week's faculty meeting.

By the start of the next school year, we had launched our "Red and Blue Crew Award." We were too late for Neil Feeney, but I told his story at every awards presentation. Spearheaded by Christine Murray and Maggie McKeever, two teachers who instantly saw the need, Red and Blue Crew Awards were given to students who had distinguished themselves in an extraordinary fashion for the very "ordinary" notions of respectfulness, goodwill, and kindness to others. Any adult in the building could nominate a student, and a committee met monthly to select those most worthy. Their names were read over the public-address system (thank you, Neil), and they received a T-shirt in our school colors of red and Columbia blue. On the front were the words "Red and Blue Crew," and on the back, the colloquial version of our mission statement: "Take care of yourself; take care of each other; take care of this place." Owning—and wearing—that shirt became a symbol of pride among our Longhorns.

The notion of a cohesive school was central to my understanding of a highly effective organization. Without a formal rubric or even a deliberate and timely audit, I found myself measuring/ evaluating practice against principle. What we truly believe about a "good school" must be reflected in our day-to-day practice—not only at a schoolwide level, but in every classroom and in every encounter. The articulation of a school's basics—its mission and its beliefs—must be backed up and made manifest with authentic and coherent implementation. We cannot, for example, espouse a respect for each individual in our community and then dress down a misbehaving student in public.

It's been said that one can tell a lot about people's priorities by looking at their datebooks and their checkbooks. Where do they spend their time? Where do they spend their money? The same is true of schools. I don't remember how much those T-shirts cost or how much time the reading of the winners' names added to the daily announcements, and I truly didn't care. We had found another hook with which to connect kids to school, and, as an immeasurably important offshoot of the effort, teachers, secretaries, and custodians were taking time each month to think about our students in terms of our mission statement. Bonus.

In my first three years as a head principal, I was working at the district's alternative school with students who had been repeatedly unsuccessful in one of our four comprehensive settings. Many of our Fern Ridge kids were struggling with addiction, poor self-image, dysfunctional family structures—or all three. As a group, their parents, however, were among the most grateful and expressively supportive with whom I have ever dealt.

When we opened the Fern Ridge School doors in the fall of 1992, we had no "history." We were living it and making it up every day. By the nature of our work at Fern, we were the students' last chance; we were continuously refining and redefining our methods of supporting them in their quest to graduate. Every decision— from the choice of a curriculum strand to a student suspension— had to be painstakingly examined in terms of mission.

All enduring institutions, whether governments, corporations, or schools, are built upon well-articulated and published core beliefs. In the most successful of communities, these beliefs are well-known by the members. These documents can't be shelved; they must be accessed (cognitively or actually) during decision-making.

Strong families are also enduring institutions. As a young mother, I learned that common language and often repeated phrases were the essential touchstones in raising my three boys. Now parents themselves, my sons remember two of these most acutely. The most overarching aphorism was, "Boys will be boys, but Plunketts will be gentlemen." If they were fussing with each other, I'd remind them, "Treat your friends like your brothers, and your brothers like your friends." In simple language, the catchphrases communicated my expectations that my children would never settle for ordinary; they could—and they would—rise above a shoulder-shrugging mediocrity. I knew then, and I learned later in my professional career, that a condensed and easily recalled version of core beliefs can simplify the transformation of an individual or of an institution.

At Fern Ridge High School, the common language we adopted was a parable. Adapted from "The Star Thrower" written by Loren Eiseley, we simply called it "The Starfish Story":

> One day a man was walking along the beach when he noticed a young boy picking something up and gently throwing it into the ocean. Approaching the boy, he asked, "What are you doing?"
>
> The youth replied, "Throwing starfish back into the ocean. The surf is up, and the tide is going out. If I don't throw them back, they'll die."
>
> "Son," the man said, "don't you realize there are miles and miles of beach and hundreds of starfish? You can't save them all, so what does it matter?"
>
> The boy bent down, picked up another starfish, and said, "Well, sir, it matters to this one."

The starfish became our symbol of success at Fern Ridge, a testament to our belief that each child was a stranded starfish and that every child mattered.

I took these lessons with me in 1995 as I joined Parkway West in its thirty-seventh school year. In that milieu, I inherited thirty-seven years of traditions, rules, practices, cultural beliefs, and *modus operandi*. I quickly learned that certain structures and practices were in use that needed realignment with our professed mission and beliefs. I became a cultural chiropractor.

One striking example comes to mind. In 1995, West offered an array of what were called "zero-hour classes." Designed to help the highest-achieving students take as many Advanced Placement (AP) and honors classes as possible, we offered a handful of required classes in the hour before school officially began each day. Physical education, health, and a variety of practical arts classes were taught by teachers who were paid a stipend for exceeding the five-class-a-day contractual limit. The issue I saw was one of access.

In those years, 18 to 20 percent of our student body was bused in from the city of St. Louis as participants in the Voluntary Student Transfer (VST) Program. The court-ordered program allowed children enrolled in a city school that was failing to transfer to a higher-achieving district. Virtually 100 percent of these kids relied on bus transportation to get to school, and there were no buses available to take a zero-hour class. So, I opened a dialogue with the faculty driven by these questions: What are the assumptions inherent in this practice? Don't students in the VST Program have crowded schedules too? Is it that not many VST students are enrolled in AP and honors classes? And if so, why aren't they? Why do we offer an option for required classes that only some of our students can access? Or maybe, I suggested, we just hadn't thought about the ramifications and implications in terms of our espoused beliefs.

Surely, I asked the faculty, we don't mean to give one group of qualified students greater access to a learning opportunity than another? And, of course, that was never the intent. Over the course of the next two school years, we devised an entirely new master schedule called the Hybrid, which collapsed the system of before-school classes and provided access to six classes for all students.

While seeing disconnects came easily to me, I was frustrated by the frequency with which I had to point out the irregularities and the inconsistencies to others. The music department, for instance, wouldn't accept a freshman into the choir class unless he or she auditioned and demonstrated that he or she could sing. "Why don't we teach them to sing?" I asked.

If a student had to be an accomplished vocalist already before enrolling in choir, we were placing a higher value on concert performances than on individual growth and engagement. Thomas Jefferson used the phrase "education of discretion" to mean that if somebody does not know how to do something, teach him how to do it instead of taking away his opportunity to do it. I was with Jefferson on this one. But I was also in my rookie year at West, and I knew better than to make drastic or multiple adjustments at once. I set about instead to lay a foundation built on shared language that would ultimately prompt teachers to see incoherencies and author the changes themselves.

I was observing in a sophomore English class one day and thinking how distracted the student in me would be in a space with such a plethora of stimulants. The room was alive with colorful posters and student work, including mobiles hanging from the ceiling and slowly moving in the draft of the HVAC. That's when the notion emerged of a mobile as the symbol of a coherent school. After class, and without explanation, I asked the teacher in whose room I was if I could borrow one of the mobiles for the faculty meeting scheduled later in the day.

As the teachers entered the library after classes, I had the mobile supported on an improvised display pole. An oscillating fan set on low periodically caught and moved the arms of the mobile. I was excited to share with them my newfound image for a cohesive school. Once the group was settled, I launched my interpretation.

The central strut of the mobile, representing the values and beliefs of West High, must be well "constructed" to support the arms of the design, I explained. The "arms" of the mobile represented everything else: students, teachers, curriculum, resources, space, time allotments, and structures of the school (the calendar, the master schedule, bell and bus schedules, etc.). These "arms" must be in a systemic arrangement that creates an optimal learning environment and an orderly school; to this end, the arms had to "talk to," or interface with, the central strut.

In this model, I went on to explain, the interfacing is only effective when the organization's values and beliefs are clearly defined and known by all. Then many eyes can see disconnects and make corrections when things don't jive. Turning up the speed on the fan, I disturbed the mobile, twisting the delicate central supports as well as the items that hung from them. The mobile appeared to be destroyed. I drew the parallel: on the days when everything goes to hell in school, that's an accurate depiction. When the building is in lockdown mode because of an internet threat, or there's an all-out brawl in the cafeteria, lofty ideas and ideals can get lost in the proverbial (or actual) shuffle. But, in order to regain balance and to recover from "one of those days," the foundational principles need to be firmly in place. Margaret Wheatley wrote, "The things we fear most in organizations—fluctuations, disturbances, imbalances—are the primary sources of creativity." If the mobile is constructed properly, those tangled lines can be sorted out. A mobile is, after all, built to fluctuate.

The faculty embraced the image, and as we grew stronger together, we were able to see issues sooner and to make changes more quickly. One afternoon, a vivid example emerged at the soccer field.

Inherent in the VST kids' school membership were factors and obstacles with which their county classmates did not have to cope. Living twenty-five miles from school required a much earlier wake-up call, and that distance often complicated participation in cocurricular activities, as well as the academic ones mentioned earlier. We worked with the students and their families to anticipate these difficulties and, whenever possible, to eliminate them as obstacles to full membership at school. I happened to be watching our girls' soccer practice one afternoon when an unnecessary deterrent reared its insensitive head.

An alarm sounded on the coach's phone—a cue, apparently, for him to dismiss three members of the team so that they could catch the 5:30 activity bus. The three young ladies lived in the city of St. Louis, and the bus was their only transportation home. Practice, however, continued until 6 p.m. I had no authority or influence to change the departure time of the bus, but I had hired the soccer coaches…

In a meeting I scheduled with the coaching staff the next day, we spoke about the language we used as a faculty concerning the importance of true membership and inclusion. When I tied the conversation to my observation on the field, the coaches were authentic in their apologies. "Beginning today," the head coach told his assistants, "practice ends when the buses roll."

These good people never intended to diminish the importance of any member of the squad, and yet, routinely continuing practice without certain kids sent that message. The lesson for the soccer program that day was the difference between the *intent* and the *impact* of our decisions.

A little acclaimed movie, *The Doctor*, explores the same premise. In the film, William Hurt plays Jack McKee, a cardiac surgeon who is diagnosed with cancer of the larynx. When the doctor becomes a patient in his own hospital, his eyes are opened to the unintended impact on patients of routine hospital procedures.

As a result, the doctor insists that medical staff change their language. For example, instead of speaking about "the terminal patient in 212," he directs them to speak of "Mr. Smith, who is being treated for symptoms of stroke." He creates a 72-hour "learning experience" for his medical residents where they simulate life as it will be for their patients—complete with barium enemas and finger sticks to draw blood.

To protect against isolating or alienating any of a school's constituencies, an effective leader must view her school through each group's lens: through the eyes of the child who learns there; through the eyes of the teacher, the secretary, and the custodian who work there; and through the eyes of the parent who trustingly sends his child there each morning. When the systems, practices, and policies in place are aligned with the beliefs the leader articulates, the school environment is coherent and accessible to all. When there is a disconnect, such as the soccer practice schedule or the zero-hour class offerings, the community must make adjustments.

Confronting these disconnects together at West High also accelerated our readiness as a faculty to imagine and to embrace a symbol that would exemplify the fulfillment of our mission. For several years, I had been articulating our goals through a childhood lens. My father would often take us to a park near our home in Philadelphia where there was an old-fashioned merry-go-round. As my brother, sister, and I climbed on the backs of the wooden horses, the music would play, the platform would turn, and a single brass ring would drop down on a rope from the ceiling of the carousel. As our horses passed by the ring, we would lunge for it. The lucky child who hauled it in would receive a prize. The practice has long ago been stopped, undoubtedly because too many children toppled from their horses in the quest for the ring. The lawsuit settlements, I'm guessing, became prohibitive.

Any worthy high school program seeks two end results (or brass rings) for each student: academic achievement and a sense of belonging through cocurricular and extracurricular opportunities. Parkway West was no different.

When state testing was initiated in the late '90s, the 400-plus public high schools in Missouri were ranked by the percentage of students who reached or exceeded preestablished benchmarks. In every subject matter tested, West High was always among the top ten.

West High was no slouch in the athletic and activity arena either. Dozens of state championship banners hung in our gyms. Our marching band, choirs, dance squads, and competitive academic teams frequently distinguished themselves as well. We were understandably proud of our students' accomplishments in all areas, and we were committed to continuing the excellence. "Academics" and "Membership" became two brass rings we wanted our Longhorns to have pocketed when they graduated. But there was a third ring too. This one was harder to define or to boil down to one word.

As the faculty, student body, and I spoke, we agreed that we would have captured a third brass ring when a West grad is out in the world—at a job, in the service, or in college—and the people around him notice that there is something special about him or her. To borrow the French phrase, there's a "je ne sais pas qua" about him, a certain unqualified blend of kindness, responsibility, and caring for others that defies a one-word designation. But when a stranger asks the grad, "Where did you go to high school?" and learns that he was a West High Longhorn, that stranger would say, "Ah, I should have known."

Not all people are capable of achieving scholastic prominence. Many are not interested in participating in activities beyond the school day, while some are unable to do so. But, if we view "achievement" as the knowledge that we have worked hard and done the very best that we can, all are capable of reaching a personal best.

In her book *The Peaceable Classroom*, Mary Rose O'Reilley writes, "The world of school is as morally ambiguous as any back alley." In the community of two thousand or more people that was West High, we may have had a dozen understandings of what it means to reach one's personal best. Consensus in defining our terms was not a realistic option nor even, we decided, a necessary one. Simply by engaging in the dialogue, we had raised our awareness and our expectations for our kids and for ourselves. Apart from any measure of scholastic or performance ability, our vision for West was that all students would be distinguished by the depth of their character.

Sanford McDonnell once observed that "knowledge without character is dangerous and a potential menace to society. America will not be strong if we graduate young people from our schools who are brilliant but dishonest, who have great intellectual knowledge but don't care about others, who are highly creative thinkers but are irresponsible. Martin Luther King, Jr., stated it well: 'Intelligence plus character—that is the goal of true education.'"

We adopted a symbol of three overlapping brass rings: Academics, Membership, and Relationships. Seen as a Venn diagram, in the area where the rings overlapped lay the fulfillment of our mission: achievement for all. We were determined to keep all three equally prominent and to root out obstacles to their attainment.

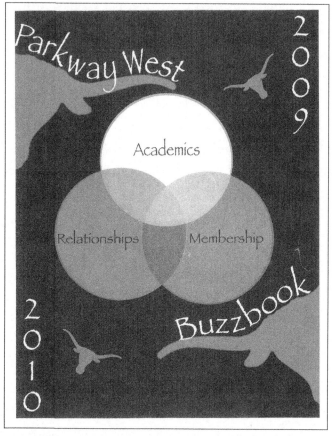

The Three Brass Rings on the cover of the West High Buzz Book in 2009. Used with permission of the artist, Bretton Hamilton.

During my tenure as principal, we got pretty good at seeing issues before they impacted one of our rings for anyone in the

West High realm. But, in the fall of 2007, we came face-to-face with a situation that truly challenged our resolve.

The Metro Transit Company, St. Louis's bus and rail system, decided to cut costs by eliminating some routes. One of the sacrificial runs connected our campus to Highway 40, the main east-west artery in the region. Darrel Johnson's education appeared to be collateral damage.

A participant in the VST Program, Darrel's home address changed several times during his high school years; for many financially strapped families such as his, forced relocation was a fact of life. Darrel no longer lived within the city limits, making him ineligible to ride buses provided by the district. Our superintendent had granted an exception so that he could finish his high school career with us at West, as long as he could provide his own transportation.

At the time of the transit crunch, Darrel was a strong senior student, clearly on target for a May 2008 graduation. Until his bus route was canceled.

I knew Darrel well, and during his sophomore year, he told me I should call him "Chicken." Darrel had been given the nickname as a little boy because his legs were so skinny. Although a considerably taller teenager now, his legs were still pretty skinny. I figured I had earned his trust and enjoyed the friendly association that the use of his moniker afforded us.

The morning after the bus news, Chicken tracked me down, he said, to say goodbye. With his bus route canceled, public transportation could only get him within eight miles of school. Chicken didn't think his skinny legs could walk that far every day and be on time for class.

With apologies to the *Apollo 13* scriptwriters, losing Chicken from our school was simply not an option. I told him so, but he merely shook his head and walked off. People "like Chicken" have faced so many seemingly insurmountable issues in their lives that when an easy fix emerges for a problem, they take it. Darrel would not be the first in his family to drop out of high school because of mitigating circumstances. To the contrary, he would have been the first to earn his diploma. I went into salvation mode.

I called Darrel's father to talk about possibilities. If I could arrange for rides to and from the bus station eight miles away, would he sign a release that our lawyers would draw up, I asked. His silence puzzled me at first.

"Mr. Johnson," I said, "I promise to select only highly responsible adults who know your son. The release is just part of the legalese that we'll have to work through to make it possible."

His response humbled and encouraged me. "You would do that for my boy?" he mumbled, choking back tears. "No one has ever done anything like that for my family." And so, we devised what came to be known as "The Chicken Run."

In an issue of the *New Yorker,* columnist David Remnick wisely observed, "If I was going to burn down the house, it seemed fair to call the one who held the deed." Remnick's is good advice that, in this instance, I ignored, clearing the plan with my boss *after* I proposed it to the Johnson family. It's undoubtedly wiser to reverse that order, but I was determined to keep Darrel in school. I then approached my administrative team to describe the problem…and to present a solution. I told them that I would personally pick up and drop off Darrel every day that I could. Realistically, however, I knew we'd need a team approach to make this work. I was prepared to pitch the idea in terms of our mission statement with a walk-the-talk speech, but it was absolutely unnecessary to do so. Four of the six eagerly agreed to go above and beyond the sphere of their duties and signed on as drivers.

The lawyers were next. At my urging (and now with the knowledge and support of my superintendent), they created a document that asked Darrel's father to release our team of drivers from any culpability while transporting his son in their own vehicles. School administrators—at least the good ones—are among the most altruistic people I know. On paper, their salaries look pretty impressive, particularly in the world of education. If we divide their paychecks into an hourly rate, however, the clerk at Target fares better.

We hadn't planned on secrecy with our transportation project, but, at Darrel's request, the administrative team didn't share the plan with his teachers or anyone else in the building. Darrel did not want his teachers to compromise their expectations for him out of sympathy for his situation. Nonetheless, our scheme was inadvertently exposed.

Each administrator carried a walkie-talkie on campus, and there were units at all of our secretaries' desks, as well as in key offices around the building, such as attendance and the infirmary. Consequently, many unintended listeners heard transmissions. During this period of time, it was my voice on the walkie at the end of the day asking, "Who's got the Chicken Run today?"

After about four weeks of our Get-Darrel-to-School crusade, Grace Rayburn, one of our secretaries, showed up in my office with a question. Pointing to her radio, she said, "OK, Boss, what's going on? Are you guys eating chicken sandwiches EVERY night or what?"

It took me a second to catch her drift, and then I laughed and explained. Grace was so moved by our efforts that, unbeknownst to me, she called the press. Several weeks later, our local newspaper ran a front-page article that featured our Chicken story. When approached by the reporter prior to the article's publication, I asked that the focus of his story not be on what the adults were doing. The reporter honored that request by highlighting Darrel's determination to earn his diploma. What emerged was the story of a coherent school community—one that finds a way to ensure that the behaviors we exhibit resonate with the beliefs we profess. The bottom line? Darrel graduated with his class in May, never having missed a day of school.

On a personal level, the Chicken Run taught me the leverage that the principal of a school can wield through example. I always intended to share Darrel's story with the faculty after his graduation. While the newspaper article preempted me, the lesson held.

At the final faculty meeting of that school year, we shared ideas on how to balance rigorous academic expectations with compassionate care in our classrooms—or in any other work or play area associated with school. Bus drivers, cooks, coaches, and secretaries, as well as teachers and administrators, have the opportunity—and I would argue, the responsibility—to provide a physically and emotionally safe environment for kids whenever interactions occur. Chicken's story became the standard for our commitment to the personal and academic success of each student entrusted to us.

Educating young people is a human business, and a moral one. Personalizing the educational experience for 1,500 students in a comprehensive public high school is a daunting challenge, to be sure. And yet, to avoid doing so whenever possible ought to be unthinkable.

As a post-script to Chicken's story, several financially secure families in our school community read the newspaper article and came forward to help. Choosing to remain anonymous, they paid for his tuition, books, and transportation costs so that, two years later, Darrel earned his associate's degree from the St. Louis Community College system.

Every so often, good begets good.

Chapter 3 – It's All in the Approach

Every time you have to speak, you
are auditioning for leadership.

– James Humes

A funny episode of *Seinfeld* (is there any other kind?) shows Elaine and Jerry having coffee while reading the morning paper. An article catches Elaine's attention, and she remarks, "Listen to this: 'According to the American Psychological Association, the fear of public speaking ranks higher in most people's minds than the fear of death.'"

Jerry replies with a snort, "In other words, at a funeral, the average person would rather be in the casket than giving the eulogy."

One of the key stressors for many principals is the frequency with which they are asked to take the microphone or to spontaneously address a group of people. I felt blessed to have had a strong foundation in speech and debate both in high school and college. To prepare us for competitions, my high school forensics coach drilled into us the importance of nonverbals in effective (and medal-winning) communication. The "judging" began when we rose from our seat and approached the podium, long before we'd said our first words. In a leader's world, communication is the coin of the realm.

I got to my desk by 6:30 each morning, but my day began when I stepped out of my car in the parking lot. I learned that lesson the hard way. As I entered the main foyer of West High one dark, wintry morning, I looked up to see Maureen McCormick, a foreign language teacher, waiting for me. I had been deep in thought, and without realizing it, I was giving off a bad vibe. My body was screaming, "I am overwhelmed and preoccupied."

As soon as I caught sight of Maureen, however, I straightened up and blurted out a cheery, "Good morning."

Maureen hurried over to me, her voice cloaked in concern as she said, "Oh, my. You look like you could use a hug."

I assured her that I was fine and that I just had a lot on my mind. But my reversal was too late. Maureen knew what time I arrived each morning; she had positioned herself near the front door to catch a few minutes with me before the swirl of the day began. Because she was a caring and compassionate woman, however, she immediately shelved her own issue to ease my emotional state. "You don't need one more thing today," she said as she left for her classroom.

Body language speaks louder than we know. My intense introspective mien had blocked Maureen out; I had failed my teacher because my body language made me inaccessible to her. That should never happen. My assistant principal, Michael O'Brien, once asked me how I dealt so well with all the "interruptions" in the job. I told him that the interruptions *were* my job. That morning with Maureen, I had forgotten my own counsel.

The winter season provided an interesting challenge for me in terms of communications. As the first snowflakes would fall, the questions and the testimonials from students would begin: "Are you going to call off school?" "I'm scared to drive in the snow;

you have to send me home." "You always say you care about us, so send us home."

Rather than hide in my office, I gamely walked the halls on bad weather days and dismissed all pleas for "freedom" with a smile. In our district, as in most public school systems, the decision to cancel school was not the building principal's to make. The superintendent, with board of education sanction, made the call. But none of these folks were in the math wing where I was being barraged with demands. If school was to be canceled during the school day, building principals would get a call from an assistant superintendent or a public relations representative for the district. That call was information-packed. We needed to know what time we could release students, what time the buses would arrive, and what time teachers could leave the building. Depending on the severity of the storm, anxiety was the prevailing norm.

In truth, I enjoyed the banter on days when canceling school was clearly unnecessary. But on days when the wind howled and snow was piling up on parking lots and sidewalks, I wanted my phone to ring more than the kids did.

At Parkway West, we issued parking passes to juniors and seniors who had a valid driver's license, a vehicle, and $60 for the privilege. There was no "test" to take which would confirm that the students could drive well in icy or snowy conditions (or at all, for that matter). And, we could be fairly certain that a percentage of kids had been driving a week or less in *any* conditions. On sunbathed spring days, dismissal was a crapshoot. Turning inexperienced, eager teenagers unexpectedly loose in the midst of a winter storm was heart-stopping.

One snowy morning early in my tenure at West High, I decided to have some fun with the kids. Knowing that laughter often lightens an anxious mind, I made a sandwich-board style sign out of rope and a couple of poster boards. On the front, I printed in bold letters: IT'S NOT MY DECISION. And on the back: CALL THE SUPERINTENDENT AT XXX-XXXX.

My snow day sign was well received because it sent deliberate messages in a whimsical way: "I'm aware of your concerns; I share your concerns; I'm here with you; now, get back to work." I also have a poignant memory of another time when a sense of humor eased a tense situation on a whole other level.

The year was 1995—my first year as head of school at Parkway West. On the afternoon of our opening football game, the superintendent received an anonymous letter indicating that a bomb would be detonated sometime during the game that evening. Our opponent was one of our sister schools in the same district, Parkway South, and so we were expecting a capacity crowd.

The chief of the local police, several detectives, Tom Reeves (South's principal), and members of the bomb squad quickly assembled in my office along with my bosses at the district level. After scrutinizing the language of the threat, the law enforcement people in the meeting did not deem it to be a credible one, but we wanted to cover all the bases.

Canine teams were called in to sniff for explosives in the stadium, in the wooded areas on campus, and, to be thorough, the school itself. Once we were reasonably certain that there was no danger, we brainstormed next steps.

My priority was to inform the extended communities of both schools about the threat, about our actions taken to evaluate it, and about the conclusion we had reached. The challenge was to find balanced language that conveyed the facts while inspiring confidence in the decisions we had made. These were the pre-Columbine days of school leadership and its interaction with law enforcement; there was not yet a category of crime called "school shootings." We had no email blasts or emergency phone alerts—most of us didn't even have cell phones yet. So, we drafted a letter of explanation and a posse of willing adults to stand at every entrance to our campus, distributing the information as people drove in to attend the game. We wanted to be sure each could make an informed decision about their presence on campus that night.

As we got closer to game time, I suddenly realized that we had not conferred the same courtesy of *refusal to attend* to the teams and the coaches themselves. For sure, they also had a right to absent themselves. I told my athletic director that I wanted to speak to our football players. As we got to the locker room doors, the athletic director wisely entered without me to make sure the young men were in appropriate garb to meet their female principal for the first time. Once the all clear was given, I entered a very quiet room. West's forty-eight players—all padded up and looking like huge, lumpy humans—were sitting on the floor in front of me as I introduced myself.

In that moment, I knew that my body language and tone of voice were every bit as important as my words. I explained what had been happening all afternoon and said that I wanted each of them to be able to decide for himself if he wanted to stay and compete that night. I caught the head coach's eye as I promised, "There will be no repercussions should you decide to leave right now. Isn't that right, Coach Rogers?" I knew I had caught the coach off guard, but he said all the right things, backing me up and assuring his players that it was an individual decision.

When I asked if there were any questions, a long arm went up in the back of the room. As the young player stood, he asked, "Ma'am, I have a question. Are YOU staying for the game?" A ripple of laughter broke the tension, as I assured him I would be there.

The art of listening is often underrated as an important skill for effective leadership. To listen well is to communicate respect for the speaker, to emphasize a need for the information that is being exchanged, and, sometimes, to teach a belief in the importance of shared leadership in an effective school.

Margaret Wheatley offers relevant support in her book *Turning to One Another*: "Why is being heard so healing? I don't know the full answer to that question, but I do know it has something to do with the fact that listening creates relationship." I tested Wheatley's theory one day with my granddaughter.

In the spring of 2010, my granddaughter, Caroline, and I had a special moment. On the prematurely warm March afternoon of her fourth birthday, we were sitting at a sidewalk café near her home in Brooklyn, New York. My son's beautiful daughter was suddenly in my lap with her hand cupped behind her ear.

"Listen, Grandma," she said. "What is that noise?"

The multitude of sounds that bombarded my Missouri ears were everyday background to her: subway trains rushed by underground, and an endless fleet of buses, taxis, cars, and trucks jockeyed for the right of way on the NYC streets. Caroline, however, had filtered out this familiar din and was focused on a sound that was new to her. I was not as successful.

After several of my suggestions were rejected, I was clearly deemed unable to satisfy her plea to identify the unknown noise. "Why aren't you listening?" she complained.

"I am listening," I whined, "but I can't hear what you are talking about."

In exasperation, Caroline dropped her arms and exclaimed, "Grandma, listen louder."

A relationship based on trust must begin with listening, not a polite I'll-wait-my-turn-to-speak listening, but listening to understand. Fortunately, after I so famously failed my "listening test" in Brooklyn that spring day, I had many more opportunities to build trust and relationship with my granddaughter. In my early years at West, however, I learned that often the principal needs to initiate the conversation in which she'll be the primary listener.

From several unlikely sources, I learned valuable lessons about the importance of seeking information about my school's history to value it appropriately. The acclaimed *Sports Illustrated* journalist Frank Deford once mentioned the infamous Alabama coach, Bear Bryant, in an article. Mostly laudatory of the football god that Bryant was, Deford also informed his audience that the coach suffered from a chronic bladder problem. Soon after the article was published, Deford received a letter from an Alabama minister (and, apparently, a gridiron fan) that read, "Whenever your mother and father are ready to get married, I'll be happy to perform the service." Here's the lesson: Don't trash past heroes. This wasn't an issue at Fern Ridge. I was the first principal at the alternative high school, and, believe me, it was less dicey making history than weeding it out and understanding it.

At West High School, I followed four distinguished gentlemen into the office of principal. Their pictures guarded my conference room walls when I arrived. The portraits were nearly indistinguishable as each man wore a dark suit and leaned importantly against an overstuffed leather armchair. Feeling watched and judged, I quickly had the pictures rehung in the main office. My decision required a great deal of explaining to the many teachers who had served under these principals and saw the move as a form of Siberian banishment. Had I researched the issue a bit by seeking input, I might have conveyed my reasons for the change with some acceptability. (For the record, in my retirement portrait, I sat *in* the leather chair wearing a bright blue suit jacket and a slim black skirt that barely skimmed my knees. There were flowers on a side table.)

The other part of this lesson has to do with long-standing traditions; we shouldn't tread on those either. An episode of *Frasier* manifested this truth for me, although, sadly, too late. Hoping to spruce up the living room, Frasier throws out his father's favorite chair without consulting him. Several of the recliner's springs had sprung, and stuffing was visible in both arms; it was twenty-five years old and filled with dog hair and crumbs.

When his father reacted in outrage, Frasier exclaimed, "But, Dad, it's just a chair!"

His father remanded him swiftly, "Sure, it's just a chair. It was just the chair I was in when you called to tell me I was a grandfather. And it was just the chair I came back to after your mother died." Memories are often tied to "stuff." We shouldn't discard that stuff without proper inquiry.

In my second year at West, I requested that the grounds crew take down a rusted iron sculpture that was on a parking lot island at the front of school. There was no marker on the ground in front, no indication of whence it had come. To this historically uninformed principal, the sculpture was an eyesore. The morning after it was removed, Laura Bennett, a social studies teacher on our staff, came to me puzzled about its disappearance. From Laura I learned that the sculpture had been a gift to the school from the Class of 1991—her graduating class. She was angry and insulted, and she deemed my behavior arrogant. I was suitably chastised. The lesson? Had I minimally sent an email to the faculty asking if anyone had knowledge about the origin of the sculpture's appearance on campus, things might have turned out differently. A piece of West's history could have been restored and celebrated, and I might not have had to struggle to shrug the mantle of arrogance.

I learned early on that a false sense of anonymity accompanies phone calls and emails. Faceless conversations can fuel intense volleys that might be diffused with eye contact. One very angry father taught me (inadvertently) a strategy that helps.

One fall morning, a dad called in a fury, ranting and raving about something that had happened in his son's history class the day before. He was so completely out of control that I couldn't even comprehend what had happened. He spewed a series of insults and threats: "What kind of a place are you running over there?" "Never has anyone been so disrespectful." "I'll have your job!" Trust me, after five minutes of his bombastic language, I was ready to wrap up the job and bring it to him.

When the father finally paused to catch his breath, I quickly interjected, "Sir, why don't you come up to school so we can talk?"

He huffed and bellowed, "You do not want this guy in your office, lady."

"Yes, sir," I assured him, "I do. Come to my office; I'll be waiting."

My secretary's office was just outside mine, and I waited by Lauren's desk, leaning against the doorframe. Lauren and I had worked together for many years, and I trusted and relied on her insights and observations. As we waited for Mad Dad to arrive, I asked her if any of our thirteen social studies teachers had stopped by the office to see me in the last twenty-four hours. One of my essential messages to my staff was a simple one: no surprises. If they screwed up, said something inappropriate, or failed to say something they should have, I wanted to hear from them before I heard from the offended party. I assured them that being proactive with an explanation or an apology usually ensured a better outcome. Nevertheless, neither Lauren nor I knew anything about an event that could have provoked the venomous feelings of our soon-to-arrive parent.

When the dad showed up minutes later, he stormed into Lauren's office, demanding, "I want to see Plunkett now!"

I stepped in front of her desk, extended my hand in greeting, and said, "I'm right here, sir. Please, come in and sit down."

He was clearly caught off guard by my demeanor and almost immediately calmed down.

"Oh," he said. "I thought you'd be bigger."

I smiled and offered, "Five feet, one inch; 110 pounds. That's all I've got."

I began our conversation with an apology that something had happened to cause him to question the core beliefs and practices of our school. He had my full attention, and he knew it. As the story unraveled, I learned that his son had come home saying that his history teacher had called him "stupid" in front of the whole class. My response was prompt and heartfelt; I would neither tolerate nor support such a comment. I assured him I knew nothing yet of the event from the teacher's point of view, but that I would be having a conversation with the individual in question as soon as we concluded our meeting. I then seized what we refer to in education as the "teachable moment."

Our emphasis on strong relationships was at the core of our beliefs in our high school. Although obvious to be sure, I explained why the alleged actions of the teacher simply did not fit into our culture. I also wanted him to see how his angry assumptions on the phone were equally incoherent. He apologized, saying that his family was new to the community, and he feared the incident would be swept under the proverbial rug.

The bottom line was that the father left the building confident that I would investigate, report back to him, and, if necessary, take appropriate action. He understood that our community held its members to a high standard of decency; respectful interactions had to be at the core of all we did. Veterinarian or taxidermist; either way you get your dog back. It's all in the approach.

At the opposite end of the communication continuum were the formal ceremonies that checker a school's year. My measure for deciding the success of a ceremony was in the goose-bump factor. I'm a huge fan of singers whose delivery of powerful lyrics prompt a physical response in the listener: Barbra Streisand singing "Stout-Hearted Men"; Elton John's "Something About the Way You Look Tonight"; Jeff Buckley's "Hallelujah." Hell, *anybody's* "Hallelujah." When performed well, "America the Beautiful" also strikes a chord.

A memorable song moves toward a crescendo that leaves its audience cheering, crying, or singing along. Powerful, effective ceremonies should as well. It's a mood that is created by a combination of elements. In music, the lyrics, the soundtrack, and the talents of the artist create that mood. Graduations, honors assemblies, even pep rallies are memorable because of the language in the script, the organization of the venue, and the talents of the leader at the microphone.

One of the ceremonies I led of which I was most proud was graduation. Conducting the mandatory graduation rehearsal each spring, however, was, without a doubt, one of the most predictably stressful three hours of my life. Yet it was one I refused to delegate.

The practice session was held two days before commencement itself; the seniors had finished classes, taken their final exams, and had nothing to lose—except the "privilege" of participating in the graduation ceremony. And if Grandma weren't coming into town for it, many would have happily opted out. Nonetheless, I saw it as one last teaching opportunity.

I was Nazi-like about the propriety of the ceremony, and the graduation practice was the time to emphasize what had to be and what would never be allowed in terms of attire. Only hard-soled shoes would walk across the stage—no flip-flops and no sneakers. The most difficult part to teach, however, was the decorum I expected throughout the ceremony—the graduates' decorum and that of their families and friends in attendance. The latter groups often wanted to hoot and holler for their graduate, drowning out the name (and the moment of glory) of the next student. I wanted them to be magnificent in their dignity and their awareness of the solemnity of the occasion—up until we turned the tassels on our caps. Then, I wanted all hell to break loose. And I told them so.

Parkway West High School Commencement at Queeny Park, May 2000. Used with permission.

West High graduated 300-plus students a year; each participant was given ten tickets to the ceremony. The park system in St. Louis County had the only facility with appropriate space that could seat three to four thousand people. It is a cavernous building with stadium-style wooden bleachers that line one side of the concrete assembly floor. In any given year, eight to ten area high schools request a four-hour time slot in which to conduct their graduation ceremony. The local school districts follow a similar school calendar, and the graduations all fall within a ten-day period. Most days in mid-May saw two ceremonies, one at 2 P.M. and the other at 7 P.M. I never wanted the 7 P.M. slot.

Despite sincere efforts to "clean up," the 2 P.M. school left an incredible mess. Hundreds of chairs needed to be straightened, and an unbelievable quantity of litter and discarded food stuff had to be picked from among the bleacher seats. The staff at the county facility was charged to do this, but we always felt obliged to help. The greatest concern by far, however, was that the graduation parties would have started at midday. It was one thing if Uncle Jimmy arrived with a few beers under his belt, but quite another if one of the kids did. I never had many "nonnegotiables" as principal, but a few unflappable rules surrounded participation in the graduation ceremony. Students would not participate if they missed practice, if they broke the dress code, if they were late to the ceremony itself, and, most certainly, if they were under the influence. I honestly never deviated from those expectations. And I hope my reader will believe me—I never had to exclude a student. Although Quentin pushed it.

Quentin was an affable, popular young man who had set many school records in basketball. On his graduation night, he showed up on time, resplendent in a navy suit, light blue tie…and bright red sneakers.

"Mrs. P.," he pleaded, "basketball is my thing, and I'm wearing school colors."

Red and Colombia blue were indeed West's colors, and it took all that was in me not to laugh with him and let him go on with the ceremony. But that is the proverbial slippery slope. If our expectations as leaders for the community we serve are merely idle threats, we are doomed to failure. I held my ground and told him he had twenty minutes to find a pair of hard-soled shoes. We always enlisted a dozen or more faculty members to be present at graduation to ensure that the ceremony went well, and our varsity basketball coach happened to be there that night. Quentin went directly to him and swapped footwear. For the rest of the night, Coach Hartman looked particularly dapper in bright red sneakers.

Other times in the course of my principalship I have spoken less admirably, albeit in more benign situations. George Bernard Shaw might have had gaffes like mine in mind when he wrote, "The single biggest problem in communication is the illusion that it has taken place." Several stand out in memory because in each case I found myself questioning, "Did I really just say that?"

In his junior year, Parkway West's Ben Straatman was one of the top high school football players in the country and was being recruited by a slew of Division I colleges. Consequently, I was accustomed to my athletic director or head football coach bringing university coaches to my office for introductions when they were on campus to see Ben. I understand and like football, and I was thrilled to be meeting some nationally recognized names in the sport. All by way of saying, I have no excuse for why I jammed my foot in my mouth one spring morning.

I was returning to my office after the start of first-hour classes when I saw my head coach and a nice-looking, obviously physically fit young man approaching. "Mrs. Plunkett," Coach Withers said, "I'd like you to meet Major Applewhite."

With cocky confidence, I extended my hand and greeted our guest, "Major Applewhite, it's very nice to meet you. In what branch of the military do you serve?"

Coach Withers visibly paled and uncharacteristically stammered. Major Applewhite chuckled, and although I couldn't accurately read the moment, I was sure I had screwed up.

"Mrs. Plunkett," my coach quickly explained, "Major Applewhite is the offensive coordinator for the University of Alabama; he's here to meet Ben."

"Oh, *that* Major Applewhite," I mumbled, totally chagrined.

Later that day, I went into the cafeteria where Ben was eating lunch. Pulling up a chair beside him, I tentatively asked, "Do you have any interest in going to the University of Alabama to play ball next year?"

"Alabama, Ms. P? Are you kidding? That's Coach Saban's team; I'd give an arm to go there." Ben was a quarterback, but I decided not to comment on the irony of his remark. Instead, I told him what had happened earlier in my office.

Dropping his head to the table, Ben begged, "Please don't talk to the coaches. Just be my principal. You're good at that." As gracious as Ben was in his forgiveness, the story was told in many different venues. Often by me. When a leader acknowledges a mistake, whether it's one that has significant consequences or a mere slip of the tongue, it empowers her constituencies to own up to their own goofs. The American author Elbert Hubbard once observed, "Every man is a damn fool for at least five minutes a day; wisdom consists in not exceeding the limit." Too many days, I shirked Elbert's counsel. Sigh.

In the spring of 2009, a neighboring school district announced that they could no longer support a program that had served a profoundly deaf student population. My district, Parkway, agreed to pick up the responsibility, and I was asked to host the high school division at West High. I was excited about the opportunity to create a new "home" for the fourteen displaced high school students from the Brentwood School District.

Michael O'Brien, my assistant principal who supervised special education services at West, and I began to learn as much as possible about the needs of our new kids. We discovered that each of the students had a personal interpreter who would travel with him or her throughout the school day. Many of the young people also used assistive devices for active participation in their own learning. In some cases, these devices were large and needed to be stored securely when not in use. Most importantly, our inquiries revealed the stark differences that existed between the students' former school community and ours. Brentwood High School had a population of 300; we were 1,500 strong. Knowing we could deal easily with the physical accommodations required for our new students, we decided to focus on a proactive plan for their emotional and social adjustment as our priority.

Sensitivity training for the entire staff was requested and scheduled. Michael and I spoke to the student body at end-of-the-year assemblies about the "new kids on the block" who would be joining us in the fall. I also informed the parents through my monthly newsletter. Our message in all forums was consistent: we were excited and pleased to have the profoundly deaf community among us. We acknowledged the challenges they would face adjusting to our much larger environment, but we also expressed confidence that the West community would receive them warmly. To further that end, Michael and I decided to plan a separate orientation program for the students, their families, and their interpreters.

We sent formal invitations and ordered comfort food. The evening began with a mix-and-mingle hour while we enjoyed the meal and introduced ourselves; then the formal program began. Our building manager had neglected to provide the sound system I had requested for the library, setting up one of the most embarrassing moments of my career.

Michael shepherded our guests to their chairs, and I went to the front of the room to begin the program. Acknowledging the absence of a sound system, I asked (I truly said this), "Can everyone hear me?" In my own defense, I did have two audiences that night: the hearing and the nonhearing. The question could have been legitimately asked, but surely some aplomb was required.

As evidence of the everlasting resilience and forgiveness that are the hallmarks of the teenage soul, one young man stood and through his interpreter said, "Actually, no, most of us can't hear you at all. But we know you mean well."

I told this story, as mortifying as it was, to both the faculty and my parent advisory group. Mark Twain once wrote, "Kindness is the language which the deaf can hear and the blind can see." Kindness goes a long way, to be sure, but awareness must be deliberately integrated into our practice. I hoped that sharing my major screwup could help avoid similar insensitivities.

In the late '90s, public schools were in the early stages of using email. We had in-service sessions during which we were taught how to use systems intended to help us communicate more effectively and more efficiently. I was nearly fifty years old at the time, and new ideas often befuddled this old dog.

One strategy we were taught was to create group lists of frequent contacts. Accessing the district's "All Users" list, I created a group list for my teaching faculty and a separate one for the full faculty and staff. Although I balked at the learning curve, these truly were time-saving devices and are, of course, completely commonplace in today's communication world. But as a rookie user of group lists, I managed to get myself into embarrassingly hot water again.

I considered my core leadership team to consist of the four assistant principals, the building manager, the athletic director, and myself. Using my newly learned skills, I created a list for this group and called it "Administrators." The district itself owned a number of lists that, as a head principal, I had access to as well. One of these, called "All Administrators," sent a message or a file to every building leader. With twenty-eight schools in our district, the list had more than 100 recipients…much to my chagrin.

One April, during my third year at West High, we had a particularly grueling few days. It was the week before our spring break, and everyone was on their last nerve; we needed no added provocation. But we got it.

Twice during that week's interminable five days, our school and the surrounding area were under a tornado watch. While not uncommon in Missouri, tornadoes are unpredictable, violent disturbances. As school staff, we are mandated by law—and common sense—to take them seriously.

When the tornado sirens blow, they can be alerting the area that conditions are "right" for a tornado to form or that an actual tornado has been spotted. Either way, school stops and locks down in the recommended manner: everyone who is able goes to the floor, heads covered, and away from windows and heavy objects. We stay in that protective position until the sirens stop. On Monday of the week in question, we were out of class for twenty-five minutes, but on Wednesday, several storms swept through, and we were on the ground for more than an hour. During these emergencies, administrators are severely challenged. In our school during such a lockdown, we had 1,500 teenagers stretched out on floors up and down the four stories of the building. What could go wrong? We knew the teachers needed our support, but when the sirens blared, we also had to shelter in place. It would serve no purpose if the leadership team were wiped out in the storm. So, we always hoped that we would randomly be spread out across the building when the lockdown began. Stressful, indeed.

But lest nature have the upper hand, a group of our female students staged an outright brawl during lunch on Thursday. We had a generally peaceful school environment; fights were rare occurrences, but this one was intense.

Several young women were bloodied; chairs were tossed; people were scared. During each of our two lunch periods, about 750 students were in the immediate vicinity of the cafeteria. And, in one of the many vagaries of the teenage psyche, in times of chaos, about half will run toward the problem, while the other half, with my strong endorsement, leave the area. School administrators are in grave danger of personal injury when they attempt to break up a fight such as this. By the late '90s, we had a police officer assigned to our building, and when possible, we allowed him or her the honor of wading into the free-for-all. But as leaders, our instincts usually took over, and we acted on impulse to protect the victims and bystanders.

After a highly visible altercation such as this, I always communicated with the school community over the PA. Although several of my colleagues disagreed with this practice, claiming it would give "free publicity" to the kids who acted badly, I believed it was an opportunity to teach. For those who witnessed the event, and particularly for those who were injured, my message was clear: this was not appropriate behavior here at West High; Long-horns do not settle differences with violence. I was ashamed of the behavior, and I told them so. I also apologized for any emotional trauma sustained by onlookers, and, to all, I expressed my regret that the academic focus of our school had been disrupted. When we limped into Friday that week, we were all ready for a break.

Before I left for the weekend, I sent a personal note of thanks to my administrative team. I acknowledged the continuous level of stress with which they had dealt during the past week, and I applauded them for their grace under pressure and their strong support of our teachers and students. I truly valued their leadership, and I told them so effusively. It was *Hearts and Flowers 101*.

In selecting the group list for the address field, I intended to pick "Administrators," my personal in-house list for my team. Instead, I chose "All Administrators" and, with a key stroke, sent my sincere, gushy thank-you note to every single administrator in the district. I laid out our week's plight for all twenty-seven sister schools. How I wish I had saved their replies. Lots of good-natured, albeit heavy-duty, sarcasm came streaming to my in-box. It's undoubtedly ill-advised to quote the lyrics of a drinking song when discussing school matters, but, in at least one instance, Jimmy Buffett got it right: "If we couldn't laugh, we would all go insane."

Chapter 4 – Greasing the Skids

*It is a common fault of men not to
reckon on storms in fair weather.*

– Niccolò Machiavelli

In 2007, I had the extreme good fortune to spend my winter break in Brussels and Paris. My best friend had lost her husband to cancer several years before, and those of us closest to her wanted to kickstart her into enjoying life again. Janice had been an extraordinary caregiver for Tom for many years, and his death left her numb. The trip was a gift to her from her children, and I was the "stowaway."

In the early evening of New Year's Eve, we were in Paris at the Louvre when a deafening alert sounded. A PA announcement directed us to exit the museum cautiously but immediately. Soldiers, with weapons drawn, were waiting for museum visitors as we entered the plaza. Implausibly, the throng's emotional response was nearly nonexistent. We learned that there had been a threat at the Musée du quai Branly, and the government had made a judicious decision to close all the galleries.

As I processed the event from the safety of our hotel room, I realized that I was as alarmed by the lack of response to the threat by those affected as I was by the threat itself. I remembered a remark by a social commentator that suddenly made sense. Speaking about the American people's unfocused attention to issues of safety and security, he said, "We have taken the batteries out of our smoke alarms." So it seemed in Paris that night.

These are uncommon times. In our world, and certainly in our schools, the violence feared that evening at the Louvre looms ominously in the realm of possibility for us all. As the head of school, no responsibility weighed heavier on me. By the late 1990s, school shootings had become a category of crime, and I was charged to keep everybody safe—every day. Although there have been attacks on school campuses in our country ever since we began recording history, the Columbine High School assault in April 1999 changed the game. Perhaps because so many people were killed (for the time, twelve students and one teacher seemed epic) or perhaps because of the cold-blooded preparation that Eric Harris and Dylan Klebold conducted in the latter's garage, the spine-chilling phrase "intruder drill" entered our lexicon.

We revamped and rehearsed all our safety drills each semester to ensure the highest degree of accountability and awareness. Even more significantly, we met with police officers from Chesterfield and several nearby jurisdictions, as well as with the County tactical squad, to identify procedures we would follow should there be armed or dangerous intruders on our campus at West High. In early November 1999, we practiced what we had learned for the first time with our full faculty and staff on a day when the students were not in session. The simulation was sobering. We emerged more aware than ever of the immense and ever-shifting responsibility to protect our children if an unthinkable event were to occur.

"Chicken Little" is a folk tale familiar to many of us from our childhoods. The phrase "The sky is falling" is believed to have originated in the tale, but regardless of the source, the expression has become an idiom for a mistaken notion that disaster is imminent. In thinking as a leader about emergency planning, I prefer to reference a different version of the story, one that has a more appropriate message.

This legend is attributed to an East Indian village and references the ominous day the sky was rumored to be falling. All the animals were scurrying about madly when a little bird was observed lying calmly in the middle of the road, his legs extended into the air. The others were irritated by his inaction and stopped to ask what the bird was doing. He responded, "Didn't you hear that the sky is falling?"

"Why, yes," they answered, "but what good will your puny legs do against a falling sky?"

The little bird shrugged and said, "One does what one can."

The website *Says You!* traces the etymology of the expression "greasing the skids" to the ship building industry. In order to get huge vessels out of the shipyards and into the water, workers literally greased the skids on which the boats were slid. My work in preparing for an untoward eventuality required grease of a different sort because even the most informed and communicated prethinking and strategizing is not enough. In the event of an emergency—be it a tornado, a threat of violence, or the sudden death of a student—a wise leader needs more than a plan. She must have the trust and confidence of the people she serves.

The Art of Possibility by Benjamin Zander and Rosamund Stone Zander is a dog-eared favorite of mine. The Zanders' work, subtitled "Transforming Professional and Personal Life," suggests twelve habits or customs that can build our capacity for resiliency if practiced regularly. "Out of the boat" is the Zanders' metaphor for uncharted times in a person's or an institution's life. The authors explain that the phrase signifies more than being off track; it means you don't know where the track is anymore: when you are out of the boat, you can't think your way back in because you have no point of reference. You must call on something that has been established in advance, a catchphrase like "toes to nose."

The Zanders' language was learned on a whitewater rafting trip. As part of the safety orientation for the adventure, rafters were drilled on what to do if they fell out of the boat. They were to pull their feet up so that they wouldn't get a foot stuck beneath a rock. Over and over, the guides chanted, "Toes to nose," "Look for the boat," and "Reach for the oar." A short while after the lecture, the authors were catapulted from the boat into class five rapids, and then the lessons made sense. Because they had no point of reference when rolling around underwater, they relied instead on the catchphrases learned in advance. I felt blessed to have had the trust and confidence of both the school communities I served, but I worked hard every single day to deserve the loyalty I would need to draw on in an emergency.

One morning, in the days before taking attendance was computerized, I was moving (with purpose) from one appointment to the next. Accurate attendance-taking is a big deal in public schools; it is mandated by state law and reported daily to state officials. They expect it to be accurate. Closer to my heart was its importance in keeping children safe; we absolutely need to know where kids are during each hour of the school day, if only to protect them from the ubiquitous temptations in an adolescent's world.

Attendance slips were posted on door clips at the time, and no matter what processes or systems we dreamed up, we could never seem to get them all collected each hour in a propitious fashion. So, on this day, I was zigzagging across the English department hallway at West, snatching the slips from the doors. At the end of the corridor, I noticed a sophomore sitting on the floor, ostensibly writing an essay but carefully watching me.

As I got within earshot, he called to me, "So, THAT'S what you do, Plunkett."

Despite a tight schedule, I laughed, plopped down on the floor next to him, and said, "Yep. But I do it well, don't I?"

The next few minutes of casual conversation helped me to invest in another of my students—and, just as importantly, he in me. Balancing the myriad demands of the principalship is a formidable task. In the rush of unexpected, and often unwelcomed, events that pepper each day, we can miss opportunities to pick the proverbial low-hanging fruit. Strong school communities, however, are built in many ways; we can't neglect the one-by-ones. And we can't rationalize by saying we don't have time to have these impromptu exchanges; we don't have time not to. All the little moments of support on the unremarkable days build a foundation of trust and confidence that cushions difficult and sometimes heartrending messages to a school community. But I also sought to build solidarity with several broad-stroke initiatives as well.

To welcome staff members as they returned each August, I selected a quotation that reflected our focus for the school year. This quote was printed on the front of a 4" x 6" piece of colored cardstock. On the back, I handwrote a personal note that referenced an event or a conversation I had shared with the individual in recent months. With 120 teachers, twenty-five secretaries, fifteen cafeteria workers, and a team of thirteen custodians, the time commitment in writing these messages was huge. The stack of cards awaiting personalization was my constant summer companion. I would divide them by department or division, working against a current master list to be sure I missed no one.

Once committed to the activity, I was forcing myself to think about each member of the adult community as an individual. I'd ask myself what unique talents each brought. I'd conjure memories of the lunch lady who never turned a student away because her account was empty. Or the bus driver who would come into school to tell me about a concern he had for a student on his bus. Or the veteran teacher who shared an "aha" moment after teaching the same material for umpteen years. Just as importantly, if I was holding a card for a person for whom I had no positive narrative, I knew where my work lay for the year ahead.

My purpose with the back-to-school cards was to spread my belief that, just like students, adults need to feel connected to their school and valued by their administration. I was asked once by a cynical colleague if "the juice was worth the squeeze." I believe it was. The cards appeared in the staff mailboxes the day they returned from summer break, representing an informed and calculated demonstration that I truly cared about and valued each of them—and that I needed their commitment to our mission and to our students.

There were unexpected perks to the practice too. As I walked around the building, I noticed that many teachers tracked their years at West by posting their cards in chronological order. That brought me the challenge of writing something *fresh* each year. Regardless of solid gold intentions, the same old message diminishes the impact. As an aside, the students noticed and began to ask, "Where are ours?" In a perfect world…

When students applied to the alternative school, Fern Ridge High School, the number one reason they gave for wanting to leave the "big" high schools was that they were not connected to anyone or anything there. They saw themselves as ciphers; they added no value to the people or the place itself. And so, one of the first and most effective strategies that we used to offset this sense of anonymity was our "Trusted Adult" initiative. We had twelve adults and 100 students at Fern Ridge High; it would have been criminal to acknowledge that we couldn't know every student well. Yet each semester, after we'd been working together for a few weeks, we asked each student to identify the one adult whom he or she would trust unconditionally with a problem. It is the *act of asking* that is vitally important to building bonds of reliance.

At the start of the 1999–2000 school year, I brought the Trusted Adult initiative to West High. When I first proposed it to my administrative team, they were skeptical, to say the least. With more than 1,500 students, the goal was an ambitious one. My plan was to distribute 3" x 5" index cards and pencils to each student as they entered the gym for class meetings at the start of the semester. After telling them how important the physical and emotional safety of each of them was to me, I would ask them to put their name and grade on the front of the card and then to list the names of every adult in the building to whom they would feel comfortable going if they were afraid or worried about something or someone. My detractors predicted that I would be pelted with several hundred cardboard airplanes and handfuls of graphite projectiles. We got a few, but the overwhelming majority of students approached the task seriously and felt comforted and supported by the request. In participating so actively, the West student body validated my belief that teenagers will rise to high expectations if the adults are wise enough—and sufficiently courageous—to ask. There were, however, way too many cards that came back with only a student's name on them, indicating there was no one in whom they could confidently confide. We had identified a need and took steps to correct it.

The real work of the initiative fell to my secretary. I asked Lauren to collate the data we had collected and create a document for each adult in the building that listed all the students who had chosen him or her as a trusted adult. Once established as a practice within our culture, teachers and staff waited impatiently for the lists to come out; it was a source of pride and tremendous gratification to see which of their students they had impacted. Lauren also created a document with the names of students who had listed no one whom they could trust. We asked for volunteers to "adopt" these kids. But the truly unexpected and most powerful response was from the adults who were not listed on any student's card. Sadly, there were always a handful. But George Butler was the most memorable.

The author with her secretary, Lauren

George was a business teacher who taught semester-long elective classes. In any given year, he probably taught twice the number of students as a core teacher, since core teachers' rosters, for the most part, stay the same for both terms. And yet…semester after semester, no one listed George. One morning, to his credit, George appeared in my doorway. He was crestfallen.

"Why?" he mourned. "Why do none of my students trust me? Don't they know how much I care?"

I believe there are three dimensions to effective classroom teaching. The first two, a sound knowledge of the curriculum and an ample Rolodex of teaching strategies, were squarely in George's bailiwick. But the third dimension, the "way" a teacher interacts with the students, eluded him. I knew I could develop a teacher around the first two capacities, but the third was more difficult to enhance. If teachers were sarcastic, judgmental, or rigid by nature, I was usually unable to soften their "way." George was all three. Yet he was standing in front of me looking for help. I knew I had a teachable moment.

George was all business (pun intended) with his kids; he was proud that lessons never strayed off the mark. The *bell-to-bell* teaching rubric was his anthem. Nothing beyond the curriculum ever penetrated the curriculum: not the fact that our football team had just won its first game in two and a half seasons, nor that the snowstorm of the century was predicted to start that afternoon. When one human being decides to trust another with a fear or concern, there's significant risk involved. I myself only trust those whom I believe will take me seriously, who will act on my behalf, and who will protect my confidence if I need that assurance. Kids are the same. Trust demands knowledge. George's students didn't know him; they only knew what he knew.

I invited him to sit down, and after giving him time to vent his frustration and disappointment, I suggested, "George, why don't you ask the kids? When you are prepared emotionally to hear what they might say, give them a safe, anonymous forum in which to tell you why they don't list you. If you want to share their responses, we can process them together."

George took my suggestion, and, not surprisingly, the kids succeeded in teaching their teacher. They convinced him that, in sharing himself with them, he wasn't lowering his standards, he was merely lowering his guard. And, with that guard lowered, they could march right into his heart.

In addition to the Trusted Adult, the other major topic for class meetings, and certainly one also tangential to safety, was school rules. Although I did not quote the sociologist Emile Durkheim to my students, I used his eloquently concise notion to frame our discussion. "When mores are sufficient," he wrote, "laws are unnecessary; when mores are *insufficient* [emphasis mine], laws are unenforceable."

The prisons are filled with people who disregard laws; to affect a more civilized society, we don't need *more* rules, we need citizens who believe in the philosophical beliefs that inspire the ones we have. We need citizens who practice tolerance. On a fundamental level, I believed that my students understood that tolerance is the essence of a democratic society.

One year, to test that understanding, I asked each class to take the district's four-page discipline policy and our own inch-thick student handbook and boil all the words down into ONE rule. They did it without a moment's thought.

"Treat each other the way you want to be treated," said two classes.

"Unconditional acceptance," said another.

The seniors chunked it into one word: "Respect."

These simple phrases are the tenets of emotional safety, and emotional safety is the best predictor of physical safety. There are no absolute guarantees; there never are. But if our schools are to be as safe as they possibly can be, we must learn from the little bird in the legend: we must do what we can.

We worked hard to build a community that embraced each member with authentic caring. And yet, despite all our intentionality, on some days, everything just went to hell.

Chapter 5 – Butcher Paper on the Kiosk

*Nobody has ever measured, not even
poets, how much the heart can hold.*

– Zelda Fitzgerald

Throughout my tenure as principal, I spent part of every day in classrooms: sometimes doing a formal observation, sometimes participating in the classroom discussion, and, when all the stars were aligned, actually teaching part of a lesson. One spring afternoon in the late '90s, I was in an English class enthusiastically sharing my love for satiric literature with a group of (less enthusiastic) senior students. The room faced the front of our campus, and as I turned toward the windows to answer a question, I watched an arc of fire run from the corner of the building out to a telephone pole on which a main power transformer for the school was hung. Almost immediately, the lights around the building began to flicker. I wasn't at all sure what was going on, but I knew it wasn't good.

Forcing myself to display outward calm despite my rampaging heart, I told the kids, "I'm going to step into the hall and pull the fire alarm. This is not a drill; we have a problem somewhere in the building. Evacuate immediately." I quickly found the closest pull station and manually activated the fire alarm. Just as quickly, I got on the walkie-talkie with the other administrators and key secretarial staff and said, "Folks, this is the real deal. Do not skip any steps in our plan; let's get everyone out of this building as quickly and as safely as we know how."

Our evacuation plan called for designated personnel to check and clear bathrooms in their areas before leaving the building; physical education teachers and coaches were to do the same for each of the locker rooms. We had learned in earlier drills that in some of these areas, alarms were muted or hard to hear. When the staff knew that a ringing alarm was a planned drill, however, I had also learned that some of these steps were given perfunctory attention, if done at all. Not on this day.

I was on the top floor of West when the emergency began. Within minutes, smoke began drifting through the halls, and Terry McDowell, an assistant principal, radioed that he believed there was a fire on the roof and that, for sure, a severely injured, unconscious man was on the stairs near him leading to the roof. I instructed Terry to stay with the injured man until help arrived if he himself could stay safe in so doing.

My "post" during all evacuations was in front of school with the fire or police chief, depending on which department was leading the response team. I quickly made my way to the fire chief and informed him of Terry's communication. He dispatched firemen to the stairwell, and within minutes, they were with the victim. The firemen informed Terry that they were going to have to evacuate the injured man the quickest way possible if they were to save his life. In his next communication to me, Terry said, "Beth, they are going to take him up to the roof where a ladder will be positioned. A fireman will carry him down the ladder to an ambulance."

My first thought was of the 800-plus students, teachers, and staff who were evacuated to the back of the building and would witness this heroic but horrifying rescue. I asked Terry to go to the roof first and have the teachers bring the kids around to the front of the building. He did, and without the benefit of a megaphone, communicated with arm gestures and silent urgency precisely what was needed. Police on the ground helped, and within minutes, all those who had been behind the building were now safely on their way to the stadium at the front.

By now, the school itself was under the fire department's domain; I was no longer in charge. We learned later that the injured man whom we'd found on the stairs was an HVAC repairman. While on the roof fixing a generator, he accidentally dropped a wrench into the mechanism, which sparked and caught on fire. There was an explosion, and that explosion literally blew him into the stairwell. After months of treatment for second- and third-degree burns, he did recover, but on that day, we were checking and rechecking evacuation lists to make sure we had accounted for everyone else.

And then, what was already a hellish situation suddenly took on another dimension. The tornado sirens began to sound. As Missourians, every person on campus that day knew we should get inside and take cover. Only our "inside" was on fire. The overworked adage of being between a rock and a hard place had facesmacking reality that afternoon.

In those days before cell phones were omnipresent, principals carried a district-issued box phone during emergencies. Using that device, I called Jim Mitchell, the principal at West Middle, our feeder school with whom we shared a campus.

"Jim," I said, "we're coming down."

"What are you talking about? Who's coming down, Beth? The tornado sirens are ringing."

In very few words, I explained what was going on. Jim was exceptional; he didn't ask for details he didn't need in that moment.

"We'll clear both gyms for you, Beth. And we're standing by to help."

Formulating the plan as I went, I clambered down the stadium steps and walked to the center of the football field. To contain the flames, the fire department had cut power to our campus, so we didn't have the benefit of the PA system used to announce games. But fear is indeed a coaching crucible, and I had about 1,800 terrified people looking at me. There was no need on my part to ask for their attention; I had it as soon as they caught sight of me.

I quickly laid out a simple plan: all teachers and staff were to accompany the students as they walked the 300 yards to the middle school. Despite the eerie and persistent ringing of the tornado sirens, we had checked the weather, and we were in no imminent danger. I assured the kids and the adults of this and insisted that they stay calm, look out for each other, and walk—not run—in an orderly fashion. I also asked that they be respectful of our middle school neighbors who were opening their doors to us. They were amazing. All of them. Teachers, students, secretaries, and custodians helped each other out of the bleachers and down the path to safety.

Matthew Phillips, one of our history teachers, later remarked that the transfer of students from the impending danger of the fire and storms to the unlikely comfort of a middle school gym floor was like a reverse Bataan Death March. His reference, of course, was to the forcible march American and Filipino POWs endured at the hands of the Japanese Army in 1942. The analogy falls apart (blessedly) on many levels, but the unquestioning acceptance on the part of my community for what I asked them to do was parallel to that event and equally chilling. After all, so much could have gone wrong.

There might have been widespread chaos. Multiple rescue vehicles were streaming onto campus with lights flashing and sirens blaring. The police were everywhere. When the magnitude of our situation became apparent, kids could have broken ranks and run to their cars—or just run. Adults could have too. Instead, they "allowed" me to take charge by listening and by complying with my directions.

In the end, all were accounted for, the damage to the building was remarkably minimal, and we returned to classes twenty-four hours later. But significant lessons had been learned or underscored.

On any given school day, and certainly in times of crisis, our children will be as safe as the bonds among the adults are strong. On that awful day, my faculty and staff trusted my leadership and the decisions I made about their safety; they stood with me.

> *On any given school day, and certainly in times of crisis, our children will be as safe as the bonds among the adults are strong.*

How we interact on perfectly ordinary days is the best predictor for the extraordinary ones. I always stood proudly with my community as they went about their daily work; in return, they stood steadfastly with me in our day of crisis. Several years later, the mutual respect on display that day would be tested dramatically.

On my welcome back card for the 2001–2002 school year, I used a quote taken from Pierre Teilhard de Chardin: "Someday, after we have mastered the wind, the waves, the tides and gravity, we shall harness the energies of love, and then, for a second time in the history of the world, man will have discovered fire." Little did I know in August how frequently we would need to draw on the energies of love in the months that awaited.

On Labor Day weekend of 2001, one of our most popular and visible senior women died of an asthma attack. A National Honor Society officer and an accomplished athlete, Lindsey was beloved by faculty and students alike because of her pure spirit and open acceptance of all. The outpouring of emotion staggered us. The fear was palpable: Why does one die so young? Why Lindsey?

West High has a kiosk in our main foyer that was built around an oak beam. On the beam is our mission statement, and glass display cases for student work surround it. We spread sheets of butcher block paper on the glass cases, scattered magic markers among the Kleenex boxes, and encouraged students to write notes to Lindsey's parents or to Lindsey herself to give expression to their grief. We checked bathrooms for grieving students who might unwisely seek isolation, and we implored the parent community to check in on their children's emotional load.

And then, less than a week later, our country was attacked on September 11. Suddenly the entire world, not just our little one on Clayton Road, was upside down and senseless.

Nothing could have prepared me to be the principal of a large, comprehensive public high school on the day of which Anna Quindlen so poignantly wrote, "America's mind reeled, its spine stiffened, and its heart broke." I responded the only way I knew how, by drawing on the strength of the relationships forged on the unremarkable days that preceded the tragedy.

When I spoke to my horrified community over the public-address system to tell them what had happened, I could hear their gasps across the building. How I hated to hurt them with such unthinkable news when they were already so vulnerable. I spoke of the community we needed to be (understanding, resilient, and reliant on each other), and then I silently prayed that we'd have the strength to become that community in this hour. The dread and uncertainty that a rogue asthma attacked had provoked was replaced, and hugely overshadowed, by a generalized fear that anything could happen to any of us at any time. How do you fit a geometry lesson into that?

One of the extreme demands on leaders, especially during crisis, is to balance their own emotional and personal needs while tending to those whom they serve. My oldest son, Kevin, had been married in Santa Monica, California, on September 8, just three days before the terrorist attacks. We had a glorious celebration, with many family and friends making the trip from the East Coast; several of Kevin's groomsmen and a handful of other guests lived and worked in New York City. None worked in the Towers, but at a time of such blind impact, the mind is not always easy or rational. With great difficulty, I forced myself to set aside personal concerns for the safety of friends and family so that I could give all my mental and emotional energy to the people I needed to serve in the moment.

As a school community, we responded in many ways to the September 11th murders, including a letter-writing campaign to the children of a high school on Long Island where 90 percent of the student body lost a family member in the attacks. And the butcher block paper reemerged in the foyer.

Just one month later, toward the end of October, Victor, a freshman student at West, committed suicide. We barely knew him. Victor's family struggled with financial issues as well as divisive relational ones. He often stayed home from school to mediate differences and, too often, physical altercations between his parents. Several weeks before his death, Victor had confided in his English teacher, and she brought his issues to a counselor's attention. Victor was so rarely in school, however, that we had not had a chance to intervene. The butcher paper once again appeared at the kiosk, and, sadly, as students entered school for the day, they knew without any words that sorrow awaited.

When the West High community returned from Thanksgiving break that year, I had more unhappiness with which to burden their already heavy hearts. Vivian Jones, one of our guidance counselors, had been diagnosed with stage four cancer. She was already receiving hospice care and would not return to school again. A woman of striking presence, Vivian was always in the halls and the cafeteria—wherever "her kids" were. And by "her" kids, she meant every single Longhorn, regardless of skin color or creed. When the Voluntary Student Transfer (VST) Program began in the mid-80s, teachers and counselors, as well as students in the St. Louis schools, were eligible to participate. At the time, Vivian was working in a high school where a significant percentage of students opted to enroll in higher-achieving schools. She decided to follow them to the county and was assigned to West. Vivian was an invaluable mentor for me when I became principal in 1995, particularly when dealing with issues of discrimination and bias. Vivian never fanned the flame of hatred; in a determined but gentle way, she helped people to see what being a victim felt like and what victimization looked like. We all learned from the amazing Dr. Jones. When we needed her most, however, we were losing her as well.

I was never a frequent PA denizen; I believed that academic time should be treated as sacred. The West community knew that if

they heard my voice, I was about to share either very good news—
or very bad news. Long after the dreadful 2001–2002 school year
was over, the kids told me that during those months, when they
heard the crackle that tipped off the opening of the public-address
system, their hearts fell cold.

Counselor Vivian Jones lost her battle with cancer in February
2002. And the butcher paper came back out.

Our counselors and administrators met weekly as a team to
share student information and concerns gleaned from teacher and
parent input. Initially we called ourselves the Care Team, but as
we got better at tracking and interpreting data, we morphed to
a Progress Intervention Team (PIT) and included the nurse, the
security resource officer (a local police officer assigned full-time
to support our school), and the social worker in our midst. In my
view, these were the most important meetings we conducted, and
I expected 100 percent attendance.

Each of us had a caseload of students whom we followed up
on from week to week and reported positive or negative changes
to the PIT. Our intent was to design safety nets as soon as possible
for our kids at risk of academic failure, social isolation, substance
abuse, mental illness, trouble with the law, or anything else that
might compromise their ability to thrive as individuals.

In March 2002, Joseph Devlin committed suicide. Joe was a
senior, and in all four years with us, his name had never come up in
our PIT deliberations. A solid B student, Joseph was the class clown

who rallied others with his optimistic outlook on life. For many, and especially for me, the crippling emotions of anxiety and fear already deeply etched in our souls were now joined with an overwhelming sense of futility and ineffectiveness. There was a pervasive sense that Parkway West High School was somehow cursed, destined to live under a Job-like cloak of misfortune and death.

We learned from the grief counselors whom we called in to talk with us that any death—an isolated student suicide or the mass murder of thousands—can trigger memories of other losses. And sorrow layers. Our school counselors, visibly diminished by Vivian's loss, put everything else on hold and routinely visited classrooms in pairs. One would speak with the teacher and students about some aspect of school (final exams, the college search process, etc.), while the other searched the faces before her for signs of detachment, sadness, or anger. It was the *watching* that the visits were designed to enable. I encouraged my teachers and staff to ask for help, mindful that their emotional load was maxed out as well.

During these seemingly endless days, I reminded myself and the other administrators of the succinct and wise admonition of John Gardner: "The first and last task of a leader is to keep hope alive." We knew it, but we were struggling.

The funeral services for Joseph were held on a Wednesday, the day before the start of our district's spring break. While a separation for ten days seemed beyond necessary, we were all tacitly leery of abandoning the support system we had created through such dire necessity. I emailed this message:

Dear West High Teachers and Staff,

As we separate for these next ten days, I want to share a sentiment from the writings of Zelda Fitzgerald: "Nobody has ever measured, not even poets, how much the heart can hold." Your hearts have held so very much this year in terms of fear, sorrow, horror, and anxiety. Yet somehow you have kept a place for care and compassion. Despite the unthinkable events we have endured together, our students are, for the most part, thriving, and that is because of your remarkable commitment as educators. I know how difficult it has been, and I respect and admire your tenacity and resiliency. But it is time for a break.

I've mentioned this to you many times before, but there's a plaque that hangs behind my office desk that reads: "Be with those who help your being." Do that this vacation. Be with those whom you love and who can help you to decompress and to re-energize. Our kids will need us more than ever when we return.

Know that I am grateful each day to be working among such fine people as you. May your heart find and hold all the love that it needs.

Fondly,

Beth

The message resonated because it acknowledged the burden they had been carrying, and more importantly, it gave them permission to set that burden down for a while.

Be with those who help your being.

Teachers are remarkable human beings. It was March. In the seven months since school had opened, we had buried three students and a guidance counselor and endured the horror of September 11. And yet, "school" went on: lessons were designed and delivered, students were held to high expectations, fears were acknowledged, loss was embraced, and against all odds, learning occurred. But we were to be tested one more time.

I was driving to school on an early April morning, anticipating the hopefulness the arrival of spring summons. About one hundred yards from the entrance to our campus, I saw a shattered vehicle. The hood and front end of a black GTO were on someone's front lawn, and the back half of the vehicle looked ominously out onto Clayton Road some twenty yards away. I shivered at the image of the impact that could have hewn a 2,000-pound car in such a gruesome manner—and I prayed that none of my students had been involved. As the earlier events of the year might have predicted, that prayer went unanswered.

As I reached my office, a Chesterfield police officer called to give me the details of the accident. Travis, one of our most at-risk sophomores, was dead. Sometime after 3 A.M., he and a friend, fueled with alcohol and drugs, had been drag racing another car at speeds up to 110 mph. The second car spun out and struck Travis's car broadside, shooting it into a tree, severing the vehicle in two, and killing both boys.

We had known Travis was in trouble. He was running with a rough, older crowd of kids, drinking and drugging, failing classes, and about to be kicked out of his house. Our PIT team had used every weapon in its arsenal to intervene on Travis's behalf, and yet we couldn't effect a change in his behavior. And yes, the butcher paper was placed in the foyer one more time.

In late May, just before we broke for summer, I called an all-school assembly in the gym. Fifteen hundred teenagers and their teachers were silent as I took the microphone at center court. I have always turned to literature for inspiration, and I carried T. S. Eliot in my thoughts that day. The poet wrote, "For last year's words belong to last year's language / And next year's words await another voice. / …And to make an end is to make a beginning." We needed to move on, and it was my job as their leader to show them a way.

Although there was patently no need, I reminded them of what a difficult year it had been. I regretted that such fear and sadness would forever be a hallmark of their freshman or sophomore or junior or senior year in high school. But I also told them that we were stronger and kinder people for having helped one another through it.

The most important thing I did that day, however, was to challenge our whole community to create a place of beauty on campus to which we could go and be reminded that, as human beings, our souls take nourishment from the serenity and beauty found in nature.

That afternoon, we pledged to build a peace garden that would be symbolically (and, as it turned out, *actually*) the center of our campus. Two years later, we dedicated the garden, replete with waterfalls and magnificent shrubs. Eagle Scouts built benches, and we posted a quote from Deepak Chopra: "Be still and know that there is peace within."

"Tin Man," one of the songs we old-timers remember from the past, had these powerful—if ungrammatical—lyrics: "Oz never did give nothing to the Tin Man...he didn't already have." The reference, of course, is to *The Wizard of Oz*. One of my favorite children's stories, it tells a tale of ordinary people who set out on a journey symbolic of life. When they hit bad times, they discover that what they need to endure, they have had within them all along. A leading educational thinker, Richard DuFour, calls this "the power of collective spirit." The 2001–2002 school year was unlike any other in the sequence of challenges that beset us as a community. I marvel still at our capacity to absorb each sadness and unthinkable event, but I know for sure that it was our commitment to our mission and to one another that saw us through.

Chapter 6 – Seeking Balance

You win a few, you lose a few. Some get rained
out. But you got to dress for all of them.

– Satchel Paige

One early evening, after an exhausting day at Fern Ridge High School, I was locking the back door nearest the parking lot. My weary eyes were drawn to a blast of red paint about six feet up the wall. Scrawled on the bricks were the words "Plunkett sucks." I had just punched in another twelve-hour shift, and this was the thanks I got?

I dragged myself home and emailed Tom Reeves, my mentor, and told him what the graffiti had said and how it had completely deflated me. Perhaps, I suggested, I have made a serious error in a career choice. Tom was four years ahead of me in this adminis-trative gig, and I swear I could hear him chuckle as he responded, "Au contraire, Beth, congratulations are in order. You are doing your job."

My dad was on the Villanova University baseball team before he dropped out of college to join the Marines during WWII. He loved the game. After Mom died, our bedtime stories often involved Major League Baseball lore. In the early days of being a principal, I felt like I was living Dad's tale of the 1953 Boston Red Sox. The Beantown boys are in the record books for scoring seventeen runs in one inning against the Detroit Tigers that year.

Imagine how the Detroit pitcher who gave up all those runs must have felt? I think I knew. Whipped? Outclassed? Underqualified? Yes, yes, and yes. Being a high school principal is really hard and humbling work.

One of my closest friends throughout our school years was Susan Conway. We grew up two blocks apart and shared many a Saturday morning in each other's homes. After graduation, Susan joined the convent and became a Sister of St. Joseph. Taking quite an alternate track both in emphasis and location, I hit the college scene with gusto. Not surprisingly, our lives grew apart. Although we both chose education as a career path, Susan's journey took her to elementary schools in North Carolina and mine to high schools in Missouri. We saw each other only sporadically when serendipity brought us home to Philadelphia at the same time. However, Susan's parents had been strong influences in my early life, and when her father died in 2000, I flew in to Philly to attend his funeral. The eulogy I heard the morning of Joe Conway's service spoke memorably about the power of being available to people you love, or in a leadership capacity, to those whom you serve.

"Joe Conway," the priest began, "had a prominent nose, prompting the scores of football players whom he lovingly coached to call him 'Hook.' There were nine who called him 'Dad.' Thirty-two called him 'Grandpa.' And hundreds called him 'friend.' But no matter what you called Joe Conway, when you called, he answered."

The sheer quantity of requests for "just a minute" of a principal's time is a huge part of the complexity of the job and presents both practical and philosophical challenges. I strove to *be like Joe* and answer every call, but I learned to strategize to stay sane and to accomplish other tasks in any given day as well. The medical notion of triage has powerful application for a school principal.

In a perfect world, emergency room patients are assessed for severity of need without regard to income level, appearance, age, or other subjective factors. A professional assessment of medical need creates the order in which they are seen by a doctor. The seriously ill or injured patients are tended to before the less critical ones—regardless of how long they've been waiting. In the best of hospital cultures, a designated staff person explains the process to the long-suffering folks who have been watching as others are seen before them. Schools should operate in the same way.

A custodian's urgent request to see the principal should be held at the same level of importance as a teacher's, a student's, or a bus driver's—at least until the principal has screened the need. To be sure, I have my detractors on this point. Too often I have seen a secretary or other member of the support staff approach the head principal with a concern he deems urgent. One response that certainly saves time is to turn the complainant immediately away and refer him to the assistant principal who is the immediate supervisor. Assuming the employee knows and understands the chain of command in the building, I'd prefer to think that he has good reason to sidestep the pecking order in this instance. Perhaps his issue is *with* his supervisor; perhaps his concern involves a personal issue that he wants to trust only to the boss. I believed that the few minutes it took me to "triage" the need established my leadership as universally responsive—even if I sometimes referred the matter elsewhere. A school leader can certainly not personally shoulder every proffered problem. But in asking for the nutshell version and by measuring its impact on the presenting individual, we can make informed decisions about whose bailiwick should be involved…and, most importantly, why.

All that being said, how effective principals should *act* while leading can be bookended with language about how she should *look* as well. In a bleak lesson from my storied career, I would suggest that dressing in an M&M costume should not be de rigueur.

Leadership is a many faceted art. There is an inherent dignity to the role that I betrayed royally one day. During Homecoming Week at West, the Student Council decided on a theme for the endless week's frivolity. One year they chose the sweeping motif of "color." Within that parameter, each class picked their own Crayola-inspired hue: the freshmen were yellow; the sophomores, blue; the juniors, red; and the seniors, now infamously in my memory, green. Monday through Thursday were designated as class days when parades were led by members of the marching band. In the "Year of the Colors," Monday saw many ninth graders in sun and star getups, the tenth grade brought an army of Smurfs and blue Care Bears, and the juniors baffled us on Wednesday with devils, lobsters, and hot rods as strangely compatible walking mates.

Tradition dictated, however, that the principal lead the senior class parade. While I did not disrespect the tradition,

I revealed the hell out of my rookie-ness. I was in my second year at West High, and I decided to go all in with the kids. I rented a bright green M&M suit. Replete with white gloves and clownlike footwear, it was quite realistic in its puffiness. I walked the parade route basking in the approval of my community. I was feeling quite proud of myself…until the drug bust went down.

Dr. Louise Losos, assistant principal, poses with the author as science teacher Gary Kallansrud looks on

Here's the lesson I learned that day: every seasoned principal keeps a pressed suit and a clean shirt on the back of his or her office door. I had worn my M&M suit to work that day, and it was the only one this neophyte had with her. When, just after the lunch shifts ended, my athletic director, Bobby Sherman, asked me to come to his office ASAP, I arrived in a green flash.

The athletic director had been in the boys' locker room at lunch and observed what he believed to be a drug transaction. Summoning our security resource officer to accompany him, Bobby escorted the two young men to separate areas of the athletic office suite and called me. Before the day was over, we would have interviewed more than a dozen students, some as witnesses and, sadly, too many as lawbreakers. Fully two hours into our scrutiny of the facts, however, our switchboard began to take calls from community members. The Chesterfield area had a score of neighbors who monitored police scanners; we had unearthed several illegal drug transactions on campus that day, and local police had been contacted for support. The listening ears heard. In these types of investigations, the stakes are extraordinarily high for our young people. If a person is considered an adult (and seventeen- and eighteen-year-olds can be), an arrest can change a life. We needed to be fully attentive to our students' rights as we set about to do what was our responsibility under the law. I knew I needed help keeping outsiders at bay and contacted the district's public relations office.

After I filled in the details of our day to Steve Quinn, the public relations director, Steve offered to come to school and personally take those information-seeking, but intrusive, calls for me. Steve also commented, "Beth, we may need you to talk to the press. You're comfortable and competent with unscripted interviews, and we'll need to reassure the public that you are personally directing the investigation."

"Not today, Steve," I stated adamantly. "I will not be doing any interviews today, and I will certainly not be on air." Steve was surprised and concerned about my refusal…until we were face-to-face a few minutes later.

"Ah, I see," muttered the PR director. "Yeah, not your best day to be the voice and face of West."

From no less a source than Margaret Thatcher, I learned that "being powerful is like being a lady. If you have to remind people you are, you aren't." I had certainly removed the white gloves and cartoonish shoes before the student interviews had begun, but exhibiting the professional comportment that the situation deserved was seriously compromised by my whimsical—nay, ridiculous—outfit.

At the end of the day, I was sitting with a disconsolate father. We believed that his son, Jordan, was the supplier of the illegal drugs the other students had bought and sold. At seventeen, Jordan had been arrested by the Chesterfield police and was likely facing serious charges. In an effort to balance this distraught father's fears, I offered, "Because he has no prior involvement in drug trafficking, perhaps the judge will be lenient. Jordan has been a decent person here with us, but clearly, he was on a bad path. In a paradoxical way, perhaps Jordan's getting caught will change his life for the better."

"Mrs. Plunkett," Jordan's father sighed, "I think you're probably right. There's a part of me that *is* resigned to accept what has happened as being better for Jordan in the long run. I also believe you and your staff have treated my son with respect despite his behavior; it is just very hard to take you seriously when you're dressed like an M&M."

His feedback was honest and more than fair. As the American Negro League and Major League Baseball player Satchel Paige once observed, "You win a few, you lose a few. Some get rained out. But you got to dress for all of them."

One interminable semester, we had an arsonist among us. Over the course of ten weeks between September and December of that year, a pyromaniac set fires in six different bathrooms, including two in one day, in a horrific span of three hours.

Setting a fire in an occupied building is first-degree arson; we had a felon loose in our halls who was gradually accelerating the intensity of his crimes. The first was in the trash can of a third-floor boys' bathroom; it was discovered quickly and extinguished. We did not have to evacuate the building. These were the days before security systems were installed in schools, so there were no cameras to check for suspects. I let the teachers know and asked them to listen to the kids' chatter in the halls for any information. Students who "get away" with something often brag about it after a time.

Two weeks later, we had a virtual conflagration in a second-floor restroom. This time the arsonist opened the soap dispenser and lit the plastic bag that holds the cleanser. The stench was acrid, and the fear was palpable. The fire spread rapidly inside the bathroom, forcing us to evacuate for several hours.

We could not discern a pattern; the third and fourth fires were in girls' bathrooms and caused significant damage to the surrounding areas and, of course, caused an interruption to learning as we kept everyone outside for hours. By now, the police were involved, and a detective had been assigned to the case. At law enforcement's suggestion, the district quickly installed cameras outside all thirty-two restrooms. We clamped down on students leaving the classrooms during class time, and we monitored attendance lists. Teachers hourly turned in names of those who came late to class, and even those who asked to leave for any reason. The usual freedoms our students enjoyed were being held hostage by a need to protect them. No one had been injured in any of the fires, yet a generalized fear persisted that this person would escalate until serious harm resulted.

The last two fires were set on the same frigid day in early December. The first attempt fizzled out, leaving only a wispy trail of smoke that was quickly reported. This failure prompted our heinous incendiary to retry several hours later with a blazing fire fueled by a backpack that an innocent student had left behind. As the fire alarms blared once again, I stepped into my office and closed the door. Beaten down and worn out emotionally, I looked at my secretary and whispered, "I can't do this anymore."

Lauren placed her hands on my shoulders and firmly chided me, "Yes, you can. You have no choice; it's your job." As I waited outside with my community in near-freezing temperatures that day, I prayed for strength and wisdom. I was desperate to end this nightmare.

When the building was deemed safe by the fire officials and we were back at the business of school, I met again with the detective. He had narrowed in closely on one young man who was suspiciously near each of the events. We agreed to bring the student and his parents in for a conversation. I no longer remember that police officer's name, but he was brilliant in his strategic tone that day. He spoke directly to the boy's father and mother, assuring them that he did not have sufficient evidence to charge their son. Yet, as he detailed the circumstantial data, I noticed a change in the parents' demeanor. At the end of the meeting, when the detective had described the likely legal consequences for multiple crimes of arson in a school setting, the parents thanked the police officer for his time and left the building with their son in tow. Perhaps the mom and dad secured counseling for their son. I don't know what changed, but we did not have another fire after that meeting. We also fully understood the adage attributed to Robert Strauss: "Success is a little like wrestling a gorilla. You don't quit when you're tired. You quit when the gorilla is tired." For whatever reason, our *gorilla* finally tired.

Through those long weeks of prolonged anxiety about the safety of my school, I learned some valuable lessons. I appreciated the wisdom in the words of the author Mary Anne Radmacher, who observed, "Courage doesn't always roar. Sometimes courage is the quiet voice at the end of the day saying, 'I will try again tomorrow.'" I gave myself permission to be human and to feel the weight of helplessness without losing confidence in myself and the many talented people around me to find a solution.

Jim O'Donnell is a blogger who has written about Venetian *codegas*. "In Venice," O'Donnell explains, "the codega was a professional guide, an escort, protector, and storyteller for the class of the medieval and Renaissance Republic. The codega met the visitor or merchant or nobleman at the docks and guided them by lamplight through the city streets, warding off thieves and ghosts and demons until the traveler was safe inside." High school principals could use a *codega*. But in the absence thereof, a plan to replenish one's spirit is an important asset for a leader.

Over the years, I developed what I thought of as an *action plan to survive the principalship*. While diffusing disagreements and misunderstandings, and certainly when grappling with more serious situations, a negative energy can consume a leader. To balance that cynicism, I sought what I called *pockets of refuge* around the building. In the words of Albert Schweitzer, "Sometimes our light goes out but is blown again into flame by an encounter with another human being." The rekindlers of my flame were predictable sources of quality work and positive attitudes. I was blessed to work with many outstanding educators who became accustomed to me wandering into their rooms in search of personal harmony.

One was our choir director at Parkway West. No matter how bleak a day had been, hearing beautiful voices raised in song instantly lifted my soul. Over time, our talented vocal instructor, Geri Rotterman, and I developed a tacit understanding that I cherished. Geri was one of West's founders; she had taught under each of my four predecessors. I was humbled and grateful for her support of the Three Brass Rings as a symbol of our mission. I know that Geri particularly valued our third ring with its emphasis on personal interactions.

As I entered the choir room on any given day, Geri would catch my eye and point to herself, asking if I needed to speak with her. If I were there in pursuit of assurance and comfort alone, I would shake my head and pat my heart, telling her, "No, please just keep on doing what you're doing." If the kids were practicing scales or studying lyrics when I showed up, it never took Geri long to transition them to singing mode. In short order, those magnificent voices were singing a favorite ballad. Their music never failed to restore in me a sense of balance.

A classroom that hummed with active student engagement had the same effect. Between the Fern Ridge and West High schoolhouses, I had dozens of teachers who faithfully created safe havens for their students every single day. Those environments were notable for the teachers' skills at differentiation and for the students' relaxed and engrossed moods. Many did it well, but no one achieved that equilibrium under more challenging circumstances than Rebecca Jeffries.

Rebecca taught speech, debate, and communication classes for us at West. All elective classes, Rebecca's room was a sanctuary for all who entered—including this sometimes-beleaguered principal. Authentic student engagement is a challenge in any classroom, even the most homogeneous of settings. But Rebecca's speech classes were Ellis Islands in their blend of kids. She welcomed all who came across her threshold. The barely articulate sat alongside National Forensic League medal winners, and under the inspiring power of Rebecca's enthusiasm and confidence, they raised each other's game. I always left Ms. Jeffries's room believing in the inherent goodness and power of a caring and competent educator.

The notion of a feel-good file is well known. Just for balance, I kept mine next to the one labeled "Ongoing Issues." When faced with a series of disappointing events, accessing evidence of positive affirmation from those you serve can nourish the spirit. One of the notes I cherish most was written by my lead day custodian, James Singleton. The lead custodian's job during the day is incrementally harder than the night custodian's because 1,500 kids are present to mess up everything he just cleaned. But James was a uniquely gifted man in his strong work ethic and his willingness to reach out to help students who looked lost, forlorn, or hankering for trouble.

After working at West for four years, James accepted a position closer to his home so he could spend more time with his own children. On his last day of work with us, he left a letter on my desk. James wrote, "How do I say goodbye to a person like you? I've watched you over the years with your students, and it blesses my heart to see you treat every kid here the same, not being biased or showing any partiality towards any of them. Thanks for sticking by me when a few of my personal problems followed me from home and made their way here. Thanks for always telling me how good a job you thought I was doing. Encouragement means a lot in this world of ours. If people only knew how much a good smile and a kind word meant, I believe the world would be a much better place."

The wisdom in James's comments sustained me on many a day etched with feelings of ineptitude. To be sure, a smile and a kind word—especially from the principal—goes a long way to helping others feel valued and appreciated, and they are often the only tools we need to ease an unsettled moment. In one of her poignant essays, Anne Lamott taught me this notion:

> It's funny: I always imagined when I was a kid that adults had some kind of inner toolbox full of shiny tools: the saw of discernment, the hammer of wisdom, the sandpaper of patience. But when I grew up I found that life handed you these rusty bent old tools—friendship, prayer, conscience, honesty—and said, "Do the best you can with these. They will have to do." And mostly, against all odds, they're enough.

On more than one occasion over the years, we found our cafeteria understaffed for the lunch shifts. When two or three food workers were absent at the same time, it took considerably longer to serve the students their meals. Kids having growth spurts need their food, and hungry teenagers can be unpleasant people. I discovered early on that just by showing up in support of the work crew, I could empathize with the students and calm the troubled waters. But if I slipped behind the serving counter, pulled on some plastic gloves, and actually served the French fries myself, we had an abundance of smiling faces where once there were none.

A dozen years after the derogatory comment appeared on the wall at Fern Ridge, I arrived at West on the morning of the seniors' last day of classes. If the kids were going to prank us, this would be the day. My caution to those about to graduate was the same every year: don't do anything illegal and don't do anything that interferes with the regular school day for the underclassmen—participation in graduation hangs in the balance. They were usually compliant... and often very clever, coming up with some "parting shots" that were harmless, endearing, and, in some cases, downright funny.

In 2008, the seniors, under the cloak of nightfall, framed my usual parking spot with wood and then filled it with six inches of dirt. They even planted geraniums in their "garden" to spell '08. A lawn chair and umbrella awaited me under a huge sign that read "Plunkett's Paradise." Tiki lamps, iconic flamingos, and American flags completed the scene. The local newspaper took a picture of me on the lounge chair and ran a positive story about teenagers. Imagine! It was the perfect tribute to the loving spirit of the Longhorns.

Plunkett's Paradise: Class of 2008's senior prank.
Photograph by Zaven Nalbandian.

The funniest prank, however, occurred in the late '90s. The seniors raided their mothers' and sisters' lingerie drawers—or emptied their own—and hung bras from every tree, fence, and lamppost on campus. Prolific signs announced: WE'RE BUSTING OUTTA HERE!

Praying that the current cadre of 18-year-olds would be similarly savvy, I drove slowly onto campus, looking for evidence of midnight activity…and I found it. Every inch of sidewalk was covered with chalk drawings that told the story of their four years at West. From freshman orientation through victorious football games, scenes from spring plays, proms, and even ACT test-taking days, they captured it all. I called for a special crew to be dispatched from the facilities division to help my custodians with cleanup. The foreman's first response was to hose all the chalk from the campus walkways. I wanted the kids to have their fun and directed him instead to remove only offensive language or derogatory portrayals of others. The crew chief nodded his understanding and said, "OK, we'll start by washing *that* one off, right?" As he gestured toward the front wall of school, I saw scrawled in gloriously ginormous letters, "PLUNKETT'S HOT." Now, that was feedback I could live with.

"Nah," I shrugged. "Leave that one up for a little while."

Chapter 7 – Recalibrating

Between the idea and the reality
Between the notion and the act
Falls the Shadow

– T. S. Eliot

We were not always at our best. On some days, Thomas Sergiovanni himself would have been ashamed. In *Leadership for the Schoolhouse*, the acclaimed thinker advised, "Schools should not reflect society, they should be models for what society can become." There were moments—too many to enumerate—when my students and their parents and teachers epitomized the very best that anyone could expect of ordinary mortals, days when my pride knew no bounds. And then there were other days.

In the weeks after the September 11 attacks on our country, the hallways at school were noticeably muted. Disturbingly so. Fifteen hundred teenagers are supposed to make noise; mine were consciously trying not to. When I sought to engage them in conversation about their state of mind, they wanted to talk about how weird it was that there were no planes in the sky. Or they wanted to show joy and perhaps optimism that another body had been found in the wreckage. We were all emotionally raw and grasping for a return to "normalcy." But what was *normal* anywhere in the fall of 2001? What was normal in lower Manhattan? Or Washington, D.C.? In a field in western Pennsylvania? Or in the school-house we loved on Clayton Road?

The massacres in our cities took place on a Tuesday morning; by the end of the week, our government was clear in its condemnation of al-Qaeda for the breech of security and the massive loss of human life. President George W. Bush declared a war on terrorism and vowed to bring Osama bin Laden, as a founder of al-Qaeda, to justice. When wronged and frightened, it is a natural human response to strike out at those we believe are the aggressors. Senseless tragedy feeds fear, and fear can yield to irrational thought. The nightly news anchors told us that al-Qaeda was aided and funded by Arab/Muslim countries; subsequent hysteria among some Americans summoned a kangaroo court that found all Muslims guilty of the crimes of a few. And that backlash found its way into our halls at Parkway West.

Midmorning on Tuesday, September 18, 2001, one of our Muslim students burst into my office in tears. Wearing a hijab, as was her custom, Lily had been singled out by a white male who pushed her down the stairs yelling, "Get your people under control." I was horrified...and I was angry. In comforting Lily, I thanked her for telling me and assured her that my response would be swift and focused. Although we had no idea of the offender's identity, I knew in my heart this was a supremely important teachable moment for our school community.

I recalled an interview with a Freedom Fighter from the Civil Rights Movement of the 1960s. The gentleman claimed that riding the bus that day to protest the inequities in our society was his *defining moment* as a human being. If a defining moment is one that captures the essence of what we want ourselves to be, a moment that reveals and honors the essential principles to which we espouse, then this was truly ours. From my perspective, when Lily was viewed and condemned as a representative of her entire race, our core values shattered. I stopped school. Over the PA, I announced to a startled and unprepared community that I was turning off the device that ruled our day, the bell system. "We are in no danger whatsoever," I assured everyone. "But there has been an incident here at school that I need you to know about and with which I need your help. Please stay in your third-hour classes until further notified."

I quickly summoned the administrative team and the six counselors to my conference room. After I explained what had happened to Lily, we drafted a statement that presented the facts and our reasons for responding so immediately and so decisively. In my opinion, and I quickly had the collective team's endorsement, this cowardly action on the part of one student was an act of hatred that all of us, I hoped, would denounce. We then scripted a short lesson with three essential learnings: 1) No one person should ever be seen as the embodiment of an entire race. 2) When Timothy McVeigh and Terry Nichols, both white men, bombed the federal building in Oklahoma City in 1995, they killed 168 people. No one challenged a white student at West to "get their people under control." 3) What happened in our school today was an act of hatred. How will we respond?

With script in hands, we fanned out across the building in teams of two and visited each of the fifty-five classes that were in session at that hour. We spent just a few minutes in each room, reading our statement and script and asking classroom teachers to facilitate a discussion with their students after we had left. Teachers recorded the kids' reactions, responses, and suggestions. An hour later, when we had completed our schoolwide visits, I returned to the public-address system, thanked the community for their active participation in an important social justice conversation, and then…we went back to the business of school. But we were changed.

Later that evening, as I read through the discussion summaries the teachers had provided, I was overwhelmed by the fervor and consistency of the student responses. The recurring message was clear: *this is not who we are.* Several classes suggested that we write a pledge that all would take to stand up to intolerance or hatred whenever it occurred. And that was where we began.

We formed a committee of students, teachers, and parents and began the important work of articulating the beliefs that each Longhorn would agree to uphold. The document went through many iterations, viewed and amended by each corps of our constituencies. In its final form, we had written a covenant that challenged each member of the West community to stand firmly against intolerance in any fashion and ended with the challenge that "action in the face of unkindness is a non-negotiable responsibility of all." As the faculty voted to endorse it in the fall of 2002, Matthew Philips, the chairperson of our social studies department, described the document as our school's ethical basis. "The pledge," Matthew said, "is our 'I Have a Dream' speech."

Vivian Jones, whom we had lost to cancer earlier that year, had been West's most persistent champion for all that is good and just, and we named the document in her honor. *Vivian's Pledge* hung on the walls of every classroom and office, and when someone misbehaved—whether it was a student or an adult—we read through it together to see how what had happened violated the pledge's tenets. During class meetings at the start of each semester, I would tell the story of its creation, and we renewed our commitment to the pledge to honor Vivian and to become a kinder, gentler, more inclusive community.

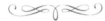

Vivian's Pledge

In response to all crimes motivated by hatred that affect both individuals and communities, each member of our school community pledges to do all that we can to promote unity among people everywhere. To that end, we pledge from this day onward...

- To interrupt prejudice and to stop those who, because of hate, would hurt, harass, or violate the civil rights of anyone
- To try at all times to be aware of our own biases against people who are different than ourselves
- To ask questions about cultures, religions, lifestyles, and races that we don't understand
- To speak out against anyone who mocks, seeks to intimidate, or actually hurts someone because of his or her race, religion, sex, ethnic group, mental or physical disability, gender identity, sexual orientation, or appearance
- To reach out to support those who are targets of harassment, and
- To think about specific ways our school, other students, and our community can promote respect for people and create a prejudice-free zone.

We firmly believe that one person can make a difference and that no person can be an "innocent bystander" when it comes to opposing hate. We recognize that respect for individual dignity and equality obligates us to actively oppose racism, sexism, ethnic bigotry, religious bias, homophobia, or any other form of hatred. Within our school community, this is our non-negotiable responsibility.

Vivian's Pledge

As is every collection of human beings, our school was by nature flawed. But as the Taoist concept of yin/yang describes, we always sought to reestablish equilibrium if our system was disturbed. We were not perfect, but we were perfectly able to improve. I chose to make the incident with Lily widely known, but in other impugning situations, facts had to be held closer to the vest—*my* vest. And sometimes the responsibility and the disgrace that accompany failure were stuffed into that vest too.

In the span of my eighteen years as principal, several lawsuits were brought by my community against the district, but just one named me as a codefendant. A young woman was raped during the school day by two male students, and I was found guilty, in the judge's words, of a "failure to protect." There are no words to describe the gut-wrenching, soul-crushing impact of that indictment. By most accounts, a profound commitment to my students was my gravitas. In the eyes of the law, however, my inaction or lack of adequate action had failed to protect my student, and I was held responsible for the violence that Danielle had endured.

The rape occurred on a Friday afternoon. A substitute teacher in a science class was, I learned after the fact, highly ineffective. He had not taken roll, he was not able to motivate the students to participate in the lesson, and throughout the fifty-five-minute class period, the room was chaotic. I did not know that I had an incapable teacher in the building nor, more importantly, did I have a process in place that would have informed me.

Danielle, and the two boys who would ultimately rape her, left the poorly supervised classroom together unnoticed by the teacher. They walked the building for nearly ten minutes, ultimately entering a secluded and unlit stairwell where the attack took place. It is unquestionably the principal's responsibility to provide adequate supervision for her students at all times, yet not one adult stopped the kids to ask why they weren't in class. All of this, including the fact that students had access to a cloistered area of the building, were deemed by the judge as significant flaws in my leadership. I had failed in the fundamental mandate to protect the children. After the initial sting of the judgment, I didn't disagree.

There was one positive angle in this tragedy, however. In rendering his decision, the judge recognized and praised the relationships Danielle had developed with her teachers and with me. After being assaulted by the boys, Danielle left campus without telling anyone what had happened. But when she returned on Monday morning, Danielle went immediately to her French teacher, Maria Hibbs, and confided in her. They came to my office and, with a raw emotion and frightening vulnerability that haunt me still, Danielle described what had happened.

I called my superintendent and then the police. I contacted Danielle's family to express my profound regret and to offer both medical and emotional supports for Danielle and the family. Because of the seriousness of the crime, I advised both Danielle and Madame Hibbs to be circumspect in discussing the event. The young men involved were arrested, charged with rape, and ultimately found guilty of the crime. What happened after the fact, and at my direction, was commendable. My failures occurred in not actively preventing the crime from taking place in the first place. And so, we made some changes.

I met at least once a month with the department chairpersons in each curricular area; they were my leadership team. After the court's judgment, I called them together to share in skeletal form the problems this episode had revealed. Together we agreed that the chairperson would assume the responsibility of informing members of the department when a substitute was in their area and of assigning that sub a "buddy" from within. The buddy could be counted on for the copier code, to be sure, but he or she would also be observing the teacher's aptitude for the task. Any concerns would come directly and immediately to me.

A focused walk-through of the building disturbingly revealed three other remote stairwells, in addition to the one in which the crime occurred. The district was quick to respond to our request to have these areas gated off. There's nothing like a lawsuit to create a sense of urgency…and it was the right thing to do for the kids.

We tightened our use of hall passes and shared "best practices" for addressing a roaming student in a nonconfrontational manner. In the short run, we observed our own rules with earnestness. But, as we got further out from the incident, we all slacked off. It was in our human nature as a staff to trust kids; if they asked to go to the bathroom, we were just as likely to say, "Sure. But come right back," and off they'd go without "documentation." In regulating this, I was ever mindful of Mark Twain's advice: "We should be careful to get out of an experience only the wisdom that is in it—and stop there; lest we be like the cat that sits down on a hot stove-lid. She will never sit down on a hot stove-lid again—and that is well; but also she will never sit down on a cold one anymore."

There is danger in overcorrecting. Among the many tasks tacitly assigned to high school teachers was to transition our students from a lockstep world of bells and schedules to the "adult" world of work or college. Somewhere between a demonical, no-exceptions policy of keeping kids in class and a freewheeling, anything-goes system was the balance we continuously sought.

I have frequently heard fellow head principals speak of the isolation and loneliness "at the top." I certainly shared those sentiments on multiple occasions, but I never felt alone in the essential quest for school improvement. Both at West and at Fern Ridge, I was surrounded by an extraordinary assemblage of professionals who were unconditionally committed to student success and thus, when necessary, recalibrating systems and practices that support achievement.

Years ago, I clipped an op-ed piece that appeared in our local paper. The message still resonates. The editorialist cited then-president of Duke University, Nannerl Keohane, as she urged us as a society to rediscover the need for "norms of reciprocity," or standards of mutually acceptable behavior. Keohane cited numerous media reports of crimes while bystanders looked on, afraid to get involved. She called for a return to the "barn-raising spirit" of the frontier when associations existed among people that supported collaborative habits for the common good. It was to hone that sense of common ground that the faculties I served were so blessedly eager to explore. And yet, sometimes it felt as though we were recalibrating in flight. Or that we were in an MSNBC studio and there was, once again, "breaking news."

In March 1999, Barbara Duncan was in a car accident at the entrance to school. It was a few minutes before the start of her first-hour class, and Barbara was running late. She misjudged the speed of oncoming traffic and turned left onto campus and into the path of a pickup truck. The driver had no time to react and crushed Barbara's black Mitsubishi against a concrete light standard.

I was in a meeting in my conference room with the assistant superintendent and the other four high school principals when my secretary entered the room extending a walkie-talkie to me as she did.

"Beth," Lauren said, "you better take this call."

On the other end was Kevin Cullen, one of my assistant principals, who bleakly reported, "There's been an accident, Beth. I need you out here. It's bad."

I ran the quarter mile out to Clayton Road, kicking off my two-inch heels as I did. I will forever remember Barbara's wails as I drew close. No words. No cries for help. Just deep, heart-rending, guttural, dying wails. And then there was the blood on the hands of the school nurse and the security officer who were the first to help. Traffic on the state-maintained road that fronted our campus was completely stopped in both directions, and most of the cars carried West High students on their way to class themselves. The kids were standing silently on the road outside their vehicles, watching and horrified. Barbara was a high-profile senior who was a cheerleader, an active member of Young Life (a Christian support group), and an achingly charismatic individual. And now she was crushed between the sides of the two-door Mitsubishi Spyder that she loved.

The EMTs were quickly on the scene, and with Barbara in their capable hands, I went to my students to comfort and console them, and to cry with them. I called on the radio for any teachers and staff who were off duty to come out and help. Dozens came. We stood with our arms around our kids until the ambulance had taken Barbara to the hospital and the police had cleared the accident scene.

Barbara did not die that Tuesday morning, but I knew she couldn't live. "Critical but stable." That was her condition on admission to the hospital and that was her condition just before she died on Thursday morning, forty-eight hours after the accident. During my time as head of school, ten young people died suddenly: one from a severe asthma attack, one of meningitis, six by suicide, and including Barbara's death, two in car accidents. But unlike all the other losses, Barbara's death occurred right in front of us.

The checklist of *Things to Do When a Student Dies* was a familiar task but, nevertheless, an arduous one. I gathered my grief team of counselors, teachers, administrators, and parents so that we could create an appropriate and effective web of support. And we asked the questions we knew to ask: Who knows the child best? Was he or she on any teams? In any clubs? Who needs to be told in private before a general announcement is made? Which elementary and middle school did he or she attend? Have we contacted those principals? How can we extend sufficient support for the child's current teachers and the other students who sat next to him or her every day?

We had a kiosk in the main foyer of West where we displayed student work under three-foot-high glass countertops. As I noted earlier, when a student died, we covered the glass with butcher block paper so that any member of our community could record a memory of the deceased or write a message to the family. Very often, the teenagers wrote messages directly to their friend who had died, promising never to forget her. As the sheets became filled, we would hang them on the walls nearby and lay down fresh paper. Ultimately, I would gather all the memorials and personally deliver them to the grieving family. But it was always hard to know how long after the death the "evidence" of the loss should stay visible. I once read a post in a Young Widows forum that counseled, "All the waves must reach the shore before the water calms." Yet everyone's pace in dealing with sadness was different. Many just wanted to get on with life immediately; others couldn't bear the thought of "normal" when nothing seemed normal. There's not one route back to emotional equilibrium.

Grief is an exhausting process—for those most closely affected and for all the caregivers as well. In her book *Traveling Mercies*, Anne Lamott writes, "Grief…is a lazy Susan. One day it is heavy and underwater, and the next day it spins and stops at loud and rageful, and the next day at wounded keening, and the next day numbness, silence."

All day Thursday, we tended to our kids and to one another. And although we needed no other variables in this maelstrom of emotion, our student newspaper was published the next morning and bore some. The edition triggered a response from Ellen Whitman, the chair of our English department, who found it to contain objectionable language and hurtful sexual stereotypes. Ellen initially approached the faculty advisor to the newspaper but found her to be indifferent to the potential impact if the paper were widely read. By midafternoon, Ellen was in my office, newspaper in hand. Given the tumultuousness of the day already, I suggested that we halt distribution until I and others had a chance to read through the publication. To that end, I asked Terry McDowell, my assistant principal who supervised the English department, to sit down with Ellen and Emma Martin, the co-chair of the department, and review the issue in terms of the Hazelwood decision.

In the 1988 *Hazelwood v. Kuhlmeier* decision, the courts established standards for censorship in schools. They ruled that school officials had authority to prevent publication if the student newspaper was produced as a regular classroom activity and if material within the document was biased or prejudiced, vulgar or profane.

The cover of the publication was headlined "Battle of the Sexes," and displayed an image of a male student dressed as a caveman and waving a bone. Next to him was a female decked out in a strapless gown and tiara. Dialogue bubbles revealed the boy was thinking, "Crotch itch. Must scratch." "What's wrong with her? Must be PMS," and "SEX, food, SEX, Zelda, SEX." Less sensational, but equally stereotypical, the girl was thinking, "Bathroom break…where are the girls?" and "Ooooh, tofu and carrots for lunch today." The accompanying articles within the paper contained derogatory references to gays as well as crude sexual references about both boys and girls. I readily concluded that Ellen's concerns were spot-on.

Before leaving for the evening, Terry checked in with me about his meeting with the English teachers. Ellen and Emma had gone the extra yard and asked all thirteen members of the department to read and weigh in on suitability. While all agreed that the language was coarse and objectionable, three did not feel it rose to a level requiring censorship. But ten did, and so did I.

Our paper was produced within a journalism class for which the students received graduation credit, and while the language in the issue was not profane, it met the trifecta of bias, prejudice, and vulgarity. I phoned the student editors, Greg and Kimberly, and asked to meet with them in the journalism room the next morning. Because I knew the Hazelwood case would be familiar to them, I planned to present my concerns in terms of the standards for school officials that the judgment provides and suggest an edit that would bring the content to West High–acceptable standards of decency.

The meeting did not go well. Greg and Kimberly argued that they were using sarcasm to caricature the differences between the sexes. They entreated, "The language used on the cover and in the supporting articles is very familiar to all our students. High school kids hear—and use—expressions like this every day; what's the big deal?"

"It is a big deal," I offered. "There's an expected level of decorum in the *formal* part of school that bathroom humor and sexual references betray." As if rehearsed, the editors' faces contorted into is-she-for-real? grimaces. Since that approach seemed wasted, I tried another tack. "Do you know the expression, 'There's a time and a place for everything'?"

"Of course," Greg responded curtly.

"Ok, then," I continued, "would you talk about crotch itch or PMS at your dinner table?"

"With my *parents* there?" Greg replied with incredulity.

I nodded, and thinking that my point had been taken, said, "Then we can't do it in our school newspaper. School is *our* dinner table. The language in question is divisive and hurtful and has no place in one of our publications."

With a fair bit of teenage chutzpah, the kids told me they did not intend to make any changes and challenged, "So, what happens next?"

Perhaps the strain of the previous few days had weakened my persuasive skills, but I was disappointed in myself that I had been unable to sway either Kimberly or Greg. I sighed and answered, "Submit the paper as it is to your teacher to receive a grade in course, but I cannot allow it to be distributed." As I stood and walked from the room, I had a hunch this battle wasn't over.

The journalists exercised their right to protest my decision and planned a before-school demonstration for the next morning.

About one hundred West students, many of whom were not on the newspaper staff but came out in solidarity, marched up and down Clayton Road in front of school. Carrying signs that announced their cause, the kids urged passing motorists to honk if they believed in freedom of speech...because that freedom was denied to them at Parkway West. I was a child of the '60s; I had been around a demonstration or two. I believed strongly in their right to protest peacefully, and I told them so. It was bitterly incongruous for me, however, that the grievance was aired in the same week and on the same road where we had stood and watched Barbara dying just three days before.

The lead editorial in the Sunday edition of our local paper supported my position and applauded me for taking a stand for decency. Lest my head swell, however, that sentiment was challenged by three letters to the editor that appeared on the same page and thrashed me for denying students their fundamental rights. It was the discourse itself that was so important. As one parent wrote in a letter of support, "No doubt, if you had not *stopped the presses*, you would have been criticized for that, too."

People do not always react as we wish they would. Despite well-intentioned efforts as leaders to redirect or correct behavior, we are sometimes disappointed. Blaming serves no purpose. In his poem "The Hollow Men," T. S. Eliot wrote:

> Between the idea and the reality
> Between the notion and the act
> Falls the Shadow

In order to process events and move on, we must dig into the "shadowy" area where expectations and results became blurred. In even the direst of situations, there are possibilities for growth and learning within the rubble of an event gone south.

The violence of Danielle's rape sharpened our vigilance as a community committed to protecting our students and ourselves. The hatred that motivated the attack on Lily prompted us to articulate our core beliefs more clearly and more frequently so that they became accessible guidelines for our behavior and our speech.

Big events demand big responses. In the aftermath of a crisis, and while the pain and shame of it is still fresh, we must deliberately recalibrate by refining practices and examining policies to reduce our chances for a repeat of failure. The recalibration process gets unwieldy and frustrating, however, when simultaneous events vie for a leader's time.

The juxtaposition of teenage hubris in the newspaper fiasco with the tragedy of Barbara's death was stark and numbing. At a time of deep sorrow, I resented having to address an issue that, in my ken, was obviously coarse and misplaced. The sudden and violent death of a vibrant teenager is universally embraced as tragic. A sexually charged article in a school newspaper gets mixed reviews. But inconvenient controversies are controversies nonetheless. The question for myself was not, "Why should I address the journalism issue at all?" but rather, "Why must I?" While it is far easier for most to comfort than to confront, it is the challenge of honest discourse around ethical issues that pushes us to change and grow.

We were at our best when, buttressed by our commitment to mission and to each other, we waded into the murky waters that churn with disagreement. In the wisdom of T. S. Eliot, "If you aren't in over your head, how do you know how tall you are?"

Chapter 8 – When All Is Said and Done

*Two kinds of gratitude: the sudden kind
we feel for what we take; the larger
kind we feel for what we give.*

– Edwin Arlington Robinson

A story is told among educators of a teacher who allegedly spoke for many colleagues when he opined, "If I must die, I hope it's during a faculty meeting. The transition would be so subtle." The stereotypical faculty meeting could kill off even the most stalwart of us all, especially high school teachers. Held at the end of a seven-hour back-and-forth with 125 teenagers, the worst of these meetings are a regurgitation of facts that bemoan the lack of success in reaching all students. Sentences that begin with "The data tells us…" should be banned from 3:30 P.M. meetings with teachers. The library is either too hot or too cold, and teachers are tired and hungry. In those conditions, no one needs to be told that *they must do better.*

And yet, as the technology of emails and instant messages increasingly dominated and distanced communications in the '90s, I deliberately planned frequent face-to-face encounters. I used to tell the West faculty that I would know I was a success when they opened their calendars, saw that there was a faculty meeting scheduled for that afternoon, and cheered, "YES!!" I never actually got there, but I was relentlessly persistent.

Teaching is absurdly difficult. Making connections with eight or nine dozen young people each day is physically and emotionally exhausting. In 2003, Dr. Neila Connors published a handbook for school administrators poignantly titled *If You Don't Feed the Teachers, They Eat the Students!* And in that title, whimsical as it may be, lies the focusing imperative of a principal's work: to sustain and develop her teachers.

I planned faculty meetings to support my teachers—to feed them, as it were—not to increase the self-imposed pressure they already felt. I believed that being together with the whole teaching corps would reduce their sense of isolation and increase our sense of community. William James wrote, "The deepest principle in human nature is the craving to be appreciated." Viewed with this end in mind, faculty meetings ought to provide essential sustenance for teachers—both tangible and conceptual. Much to my building manager's dismay, I wanted the chairs arranged in concentric circles so that we could see each other when we spoke. Trust needs all the senses. When a teacher stood to support an opinion or to offer a new perspective, I asked her to first state her name and her role in our school: "I'm Kate Corsale, and I teach sophomore English." Self-affirmations are important, and they invite colleagues to become allies. Listening to Kate, for instance, the geometry teacher who is convinced that the current sophomore class are direct descendants of the devil might choose to start up a conversation with her privately. There is, after all, strength in numbers.

In her book *A Short Guide to a Happy Life*, Anna Quindlen writes, "I got a fortune cookie that said, 'To remember is to understand.' I have never forgotten it. A good judge remembers what it was like to be a lawyer. A good editor remembers being a writer. A good parent remembers what it was like to be a child." Quindlen's observation challenges folks whose paths cross in life to be empathetic with each other by recalling the walk they themselves had in their shoes. To Quindlen's notion, I could certainly add that a good administrator remembers what it was like to be a teacher.

In the triangular relationship that emerges among teachers, parents and their children, and administrators, I felt fortunate to be well-versed in all three worlds. But not everyone comes to the fray having spent time in the other party's sphere. Most parents are neither teachers nor administrators; a good many administrators and teachers are not parents. One of the most essential roles that a school leader must master—and one that will not be mitigated by time and change—is that of decoder or interpreter for both parents and teachers; we must explain people to each other.

In the give-and-take that the quest for common ground demands, all participants need to feel heard and understood. Effective principals learn to shift their weight on contentious issues and to persuade others to do the same. But the process of doing so can be a slog. It helps, I believe, to understand the pressure points and the priorities of everyone involved in an issue. We often learn more about what motivates us as individuals when we are most in need of support. As the assistant principals and I visited classrooms and conferenced with teachers about their craft, we could see patterns of successful strategies and areas of needed growth. Frequently, and not surprisingly, the most insightful input, however, came from the teachers themselves.

Regardless of how passionate I was to create a collegial rather than a confrontational climate between teachers and administrators, there were always a few (on both sides of the equation) who saw schools built on an "us" and "them" dichotomy. I could not read the pulse of these resistors, but their colleagues could. I was blessed to have had many teachers who felt comfortable coming unannounced to my office to share a concern or to air a gripe of their own or one that was circulating. The Swiss psychiatrist Carl Jung's words were in my head as I listened during these sessions: "You can exert no influence if you are not susceptible to influence." It is certainly more expedient to make decisions without input, but hoarding that power fractures the essential relationships that a coherent school should want for itself. At West High, I owed a tremendous debt to two teachers in particular for guiding me in my quest to support teachers authentically.

Emma Martin and Christine Daly were, at different points in their careers, formal, "titled" leaders, but they were always big-picture thinkers. They were my list makers. Thoughtful and thorough professionals, they would schedule their time with me so they could be sure to cover the gamut of issues currently on their dashboard. Emma taught English; Christine, math. They were not a team; they didn't visit together. Their classrooms were about as far apart physically as they could be in the West High building, and their daily interactions were in completely different subsets of teachers and students. What made our conversations so valuable to me was that Emma's discussion items usually mirrored Christine's, doubling the incisiveness of their points of view. Both had embraced our Three Brass Rings vision for West and saw it as their responsibility to shoulder the weight of reaching those ideals within every aspect of our school's work.

Not surprisingly, both Emma and Christine were highly effective classroom teachers. They did for each student in their charge precisely what they did for me: they framed an issue in terms of their genuine concern for each person's success; they defined the issue clearly and provided context; and, most importantly, they offered solutions. Abraham Lincoln once observed, "He has the right to criticize who has the heart to help." Emma and Christine would have made the Illinois lawyer proud. Highly effective teachers—and I proudly supervised dozens of them—always sought to reflect the school's mission and vision in their classroom, in their lessons, and within their relationships. A very special few, most notably Emma Martin and Christine Daly, helped me to see implications that could transcend the smaller domain of the classroom and effect widespread change. Their input fashioned agendas for meetings, directed small-group discussions, and prompted professional development opportunities for their peers. Whatever impact I may have had on the growth of my teachers and the strengthening of our community would have been significantly reduced without their influence. They have my forever gratitude.

For many educators, teacher-parent communication is a pressure point. Teachers can feel wildly outnumbered and significantly under-armed when challenged by a parent about a classroom practice or a grade in course. And, too often, parents become aggressive and offensive when questioning a decision. The essential rule of engagement on which I insisted was simple: presume good. Hear each other out respectfully but withhold judgment until all sides of an issue have been aired. Through my role as "interpreter" for the people I served, I became keenly aware of the veracity in Henry Wadsworth Longfellow's words: "Every man has his secret sorrows which the world knows not; and often times we call a man cold when he is only sad." A principal knows more than her fair share of her constituents' "sorrows" while others in the school community are unaware. Through legal command, by accident, or confided in with trust, I knew of fierce custody battles, bitter divorces, financial collapses, miscarriages, heartaches, and cancer diagnoses in every corner of our community. These are the powerful but invisible influences on the tone of a conversation. Most parents and teachers want only what is best and just for their children or students. Yet life events confound and distract all of us from managing situations as calmly or as objectively as we know we should.

To bridge the gap in understanding for teachers and parents alike, I offered the wise observation of Elizabeth Stone. Stone is a Fordham University professor who often comments on the intricacies of relationships within families. Her words should guide our understanding of a parent's voice at the conference table:

"Making the decision to have a child—it is momentous. It is to decide forever to have your heart go walking around outside your body." The visual that Stone's observation created often helped teachers to choose their words more carefully when describing a child's efforts in class. The role that language plays in the interdependent relationship between parents and teachers is huge. Thoughtfulness often served to neutralize a parent's untoward fears for his child's future.

Every year I facilitated an optional workshop for my staff that I called "Managing Difficult Communications." The room was always full. My goal was to help participants (and there were as many secretaries and support staff as teachers some years) to build very practical communication skills in order to convey meaning without judgment. I would draw a T-chart on a white board with the headings: "What I REALLY Want to Say" followed by "What I Will Say." The teachers and staff did all the work themselves. Filling out the left side of the board was cathartic and flowed easily: "She's just lazy." "He couldn't care less about my class." "He thinks he's smarter than everyone else." And so on. The important mind-stretching work came in getting behind those accusatory and summary statements to discover possible motivating factors. For example, no parent will ever hear the words, "He's lazy," objectively. But if we say, "I believe your child has potential we're not yet tapping into," we have a conversation starter. "She's stupid" fans flames. "Something's getting in the way of her learning" encourages the essential partnership that parents and teachers must forge. To illustrate this point, I often shared the story of Jerry Morrison.

Cindy Nevilles, a colleague of mine, spoke at Jerry Morrison's funeral. Jerry was her dad, and the story she chose to tell in her eulogy revealed a lesson from which all of us can benefit. Her dad was a passionate, if mediocre, football player who retired from the game after high school graduation. One of Jerry's teammates, however, did not. Y. A. Tittle went on to play college ball at Louisiana State University and had a Hall of Fame career in the National Football League. When Tittle retired in 1964, he was the all-time leading passer in the NFL. His records have since been broken by the likes of Tom Brady, Drew Brees, and a dozen others, but from a speech Tittle gave at a high school reunion one year, Cindy shared these words. Tittle credited his success as a professional football player to his days on the high school gridiron. "It was just this simple," Tittle explained. "Jerry Morrison and the rest of the offensive line didn't know how to block, so Coach said I had to learn to pass." The best teachers choose to diversify their expectations and modify their required tasks in an effort to showcase each child's worth.

Charlie Brown of *Peanuts* fame is the quintessential optimist. Despite hundreds of failed attempts to kick the football, Charlie gallantly steps up to the task when asked, refusing to blame his lack of success on something somebody else has done (cue Lucy). When Charles Schultz, Charlie Brown's creator, died within hours of the legendary Dallas Cowboys football coach Tom Landry, a journalist drew a poignant and unexpected connection between the two.

The poignant cartoon by John Sherffius. Courtesy of the Charles M. Schulz Museum and Research Center, Santa Rosa, California.

John Sherffius sketched an editorial cartoon about the two deaths that was syndicated nationally. In a cloud-filled, ethereal setting, a kneeling Tom Landry holds the football for Charlie Brown who confidently kicks it airborne. A picture is indeed worth a thousand words. When persistence and hope meet up with compassion and skill, a bond of trust is formed, and amazing things can happen. Schools where compassionate care is wedded to academic achievement are filled with Tom Landrys. At West, we had Carly Tanner. According to her paycheck, Carly was a guidance counselor in our building, but she was so much more.

Ideals are just ideas until hard work and inspired thinking pressure them into reality. Carly Tanner was not alone in her commitment to see the Three Brass Rings manifested, but she was singular in her steadfastness and tenacity in making it so. As chairperson of our counseling department, Carly modeled advocacy for every student. All the wheels got oiled on Tanner's watch, not just the squeaky ones. Beyond her formal duties, Carly also sponsored WOW, a leadership club for the young women of West, and in this capacity, her leadership and influence were also deeply felt.

In 1995, a small nonprofit organization started a movement near Denver, Colorado. Hoping to increase the kindness quotient in our world, the Random Acts of Kindness (RAK) Foundation promoted a pay-it-forward mentality of thoughtfulness and generosity of spirit. The effort spread quickly and recommended that people participate by extending unexpected gestures of kindness: pay for a stranger's coffee, bring muffins to colleagues, wash your mother's car. Shortly thereafter, Random Acts of Kindness Day was established and celebrated on February 17 each year. At West High, Carly and her WOW group took up the challenge and began a letter-writing campaign of kindness that literally transformed our culture.

In its first year of implementation, the Random Acts of Kindness letters were just that: random. All members of the community were invited to pick up a form in the counseling office on which to write a message of support, appreciation, admiration, or gratitude to another person at West. When these modicums of joy were delivered by the WOW girls on February 17, the fortunate recipients, about 20 percent of our community, were deeply moved. Carly Tanner saw the impact and knew how to expand and deepen the sense of belonging the messages spawned.

The following year, everyone—*everyone*—received at least one note on Random Acts of Kindness Day. The message was clear: each person at West is significant; each person matters; each person is valued. The WOW girls, and countless other volunteers from across the building, worked tirelessly with class lists and staffing sheets to be sure there was a note in every hand that morning. Was it a perfect system? Of course not. Some people had thirteen letters delivered to them; some who received a somewhat "generic" note scoffed. Yet WOW, acting as part of the institution itself, was walking the talk and practicing what we preached. As an official "arm" of West High, they showed us the feasibility and the desirability of total inclusion. I imitated the gesture in my principal's newsletter each spring. Influenced by the Random Acts of Kindness effort, I would ask the parents to consider writing an email or an old-fashioned pen-and-paper note to an adult on campus who had influenced or supported their children. Unexpected gestures of kindness stay long in the heart, and they grow exponentially.

The pressure point for kids at West was in balancing the influence of their parents, their peers, and their teachers when making personal decisions. Of all the constituencies in our community, the kids themselves were the ones most frequently caught in the crosshairs of conflicting input. Most of the time, they made us proud.

One Saturday morning, I came to West to watch a girls' track meet. A relay race was in progress as I entered the stadium. Settling in, I observed what I thought was the finish of the race; runners who had completed their laps gathered near the timers in a familiar stance, and other athletes began to assemble for the next event. A full minute later, however, a young athlete rounded the bend and headed down the home stretch toward the finish line. As she did, the most remarkable things happened. A hush came over the stadium, the track cleared, and the students in the stands—competitors and supporters from six different area high schools—stood and cheered as one. The object of their enthusiastic ovation was a young woman with Down syndrome who finished a full lap and a half behind the field. I was as impressed and moved by the athlete's tenacity as I was with the audience's spontaneous recognition of her courage. Observers were blessed with an extraordinary example of sport and life and kids at their best. Reflecting on the moment later, I remembered a note written by a graduating senior's mom a few years back. In it, she thanked our staff at Fern Ridge for providing an environment where her daughter "could explore her possibilities, retain her individuality, and develop the character, strengths, and talents that will be with her throughout her life." These are the optimal conditions we want for all our children, and they were perfectly exemplified on the track that morning. This was human kindness, unrecorded, mostly unobserved, but as pure and unrehearsed as it could be.

The teachers I had the privilege of working with year after year did so much to support and to protect kids every day; a well-designed lesson plan that allowed each student to access learning in his own mode was the primary and most visible safety plan. Somewhere along my path, a mentor or a graduate professor cautioned (and I'm paraphrasing), "Given a choice between looking stupid or acting out, most teenagers are going to act out. So, don't set them up to look stupid in front of their peers." We did our best, but in the end, Matthew Quick got it right. In his novel *The Silver Linings Playbook*, Quick wrote, "The world will break your heart ten ways to Sunday, that's guaranteed." And in the world of school, kids will too.

At the end of the last lunch shift one spring day in 2002, the cafeteria became a battleground. It was the last week of classes for seniors, and the rumor mill had been churning about a possible food fight. We spent days talking to kids, looking for the would-be leaders, and cajoling all not to finish their days at West in disgrace. I was right there, standing in the middle of the cafeteria annex where the seniors sat, and "they" did it anyway. In a flash, tables were flipped over and used as shields; applesauce and pudding cups were opened and tossed like grenades around the room. In a hailstorm of raw eggs breaking around them, kids screamed and fled like victims of an enemy attack. I knew how and why the food fight happened, but I was heartbroken anyway.

Despite strong relationships with me, a schoolwide emphasis on respectful interactions, and a proper family upbringing, they were teenagers who in any given moment might (and did) choose behaviors they knew full well were wrong. Damn the consequences. Was it a rite of passage? Maybe. Some form of rebellion is almost inevitable, I guess. As the cafeteria emptied, the full extent of the wreckage became apparent. My kitchen chief and her crew, who had been cowering behind the kitchen counters, walked slowly into the room, looking incredulously at me for an explanation. As a leader, I knew I had to frame this incident for everyone so that all hope for a civilized society at West wouldn't be lost in a few minutes of savagery by a handful of miscreants.

My tears were flowing as I sat in disbelief amid the shambles, searching for words that would condemn the actions of a few and restore hope and confidence in our mission for the rest. Suddenly, Barbara, my kitchen chief, pointed toward the corridor doors and said, "Beth, look."

Turning, I saw dozens of my students walking tentatively toward me, gawking horrified at the disastrous ruin their lunchroom had become. After explaining to their sixth-hour teachers what had happened, the kids asked their teachers to release them from classes to be present with me, to atone for the misbehavior of their classmates, and to help wash away the detritus. For all I knew, the leaders of the free-for-all might have been among those who came to help. In my heart, I hoped so. At a moment when I felt the Three Brass Rings themselves had been metaphorically crushed and broken in the melee, these magnificent teenagers restored my resolve in our mission. I learned that day that if we share our own grief and disappointment when a trust is broken, we can begin almost immediately to reestablish the bond. Such is the work of a true community.

One of the constant stressors in a teacher's life is the appearance of a "new initiative." At the mere mention of the phrase, shuddering can be heard in faculty lounges across the globe. New initiatives are almost universally focused on raising student achievement; the educators I've known have no beef with their intent. The teachers' issue is that initiatives never seem to go away—there is no shelf life, only an accumulation of mandates that appear to be duplicative in nature and overstuff an already stuffed syllabus. The plaintive wail is, "Take something off our plates before you add to them."

In the first decade of the 2000s, public school teachers felt particularly inundated. The No Child Left Behind (NCLB) Act became law in 2001. NCLB was an act of Congress that reauthorized the Elementary and Secondary Education Act and issued in a significant number of accountability measures and mandates, including state testing. Michael O'Brien, one of my assistant principals in those years, was gifted at creating visuals that helped with problem analysis by illustrating the depth and breadth of an issue. To help all of us understand how the new mandates fit into what we were already doing, Michael drafted a document he called "A Framework for Analyzing the Context of Education." Across the top of the document, Michael listed four categories of our work: Curriculum, Assessment, Instruction, and Problem Solving. The vertical axis supplied the origins of initiatives or directives: Federal/State, District, Building, or Classroom. Completing the chart allowed us to see exactly how each variable on the left of the framework would impact our work as defined in the categories at the top.

I remember the relief when, after filling in the framework, we could see that in many cases, we were already doing the work now "required" of all school districts. Data would need to be collected and submitted to the state for review, which was all new and cumbersome, to be sure, but as administrators, we vowed to keep that work away from the classroom teacher as much as possible. This was, however, our new reality, and we would embrace it together. Lisa Wingate's work of fiction, *Before We Were Yours*, did not appear in our literary world until 2017, but I can apply her wisdom retroactively to the changes NCLB evoked.

Wingate's novel is based on a real-life story, and in it she observes, "Life is not unlike cinema. Each scene has its own music, and the music is created for the scene, woven to it in ways we do not understand. No matter how much we love the melody of a bygone day or imagine the song of a future one, we must dance within the music of today, or we will always be out of step, stumbling around in something that doesn't suit the moment." I suggest that the "music" in this metaphor represents the expectations for our work that are dictated by others. If we cannot independently choose the dimensions of our work with kids, as we could to some extent in bygone days, we must accept the music that is playing and find a way to dance with it. And it is the principal's job to lead that dance.

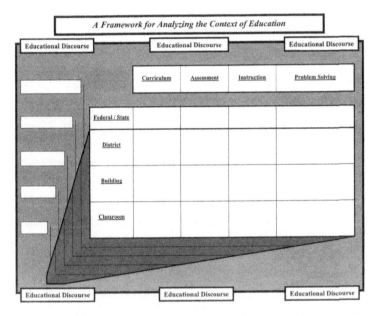

A Framework for Analyzing the Context of Education.
Used with permission.

When COVID-19 upended our world in the spring of 2020, the music changed once again, more dramatically than at any other time in the history of education. The pandemic dwarfed all legislation in its impact on schools. We were baptized by fire with the notions of synchronous and asynchronous learning, meeting our students in Zoom rooms instead of classrooms.

The teaching profession is unique in the many faceted ways its practitioners interact with their "clients." At the high school level in Missouri, teachers are required to have 3,915 minutes of contact time with a student in order to award a .5 credit toward graduation. That's more than sixty-five hours of instruction each semester. Few lawyers or doctors ever have that much billable time with people they serve. The pandemic, of course, negated that requirement because genuine contact time between a teacher and his or her students simply could not be measured when learning was distanced to prevent contagion. To be sure, COVID-19, and fears about possible future pandemics, may forever change the landscape of the schoolhouse.

One might reasonably ask if the stories and the lessons I have discussed have relevance in the face of such powerful external forces. The background against which my stories are told reveal a range of events and emotions that create a visceral connection among those who share a sustained period of time together. This is an alliance that rarely occurs in other professions. Perhaps, in the face of the ultimate obstruction, when all that we know how to do seems muzzled, perhaps then we can see more clearly than ever the essence of what teachers and administrators are charged to accomplish.

I think Lee Iacocca, Chrysler's iconic CEO, got it right when he said, "In a completely rational society, the best of us would be teachers and the rest of us would have to settle for something less, because passing civilization along from one generation to the next ought to be the highest honor and the highest responsibility anyone could have." Especially in these days of turmoil, when our society is being rocked by unprecedented disease, social unrest, and highly divisive political rhetoric, the classroom may be the crucial matrix for transitioning to a new order.

The other answer to the relevancy question lies in the contrast with the stories I didn't tell. Stories about the public relations nightmare when asbestos had to be abated in the building, for example. Or the multiple instances of disgust when a sewer line backed up inside the cafeteria. Or the gratuitous inconvenience when a water main broke. These were all part of the game as well, but they were merely situations that had to be managed and, if managed effectively, bore no threat to human health, psyche, or safety. The angst, fear, joy, and gratitude shared during years together in a schoolhouse force an intimacy, a rhythm, and a dependency that might not have occurred otherwise. And, within those interactions, are the lessons that endure.

Notes

Adams, Henry (1838–1918)

Adams was an American historian and a member of the Adams historical family, descendant of two United States presidents. He authored *The Education of Henry Adams* in 1907.

Bligh, Anna (b. 1960)

Bligh is a lobbyist and former Australian politician who served as the thirty-seventh Premier of Queensland from 2007–2012 as the leader of the Labor Party.

Boulanger, Nadia (1887–1979)

Boulanger was a conductor, organist, and one of the most influential teachers of musical composition of the twentieth century. She was the first woman to conduct an entire program of the Royal Philharmonic in London.

Brown, Brené (b. 1965)

Brown is an American researcher, professor, lecturer, author, and podcast host. She is known for her research on shame, vulnerability, and leadership. Among Brown's works are *The Gifts of Imperfection* (2010), *Daring Greatly* (2012), and *Dare to Lead* (2018).

Buffett, Jimmy (b. 1946)

Buffett is an American singer-songwriter, musician, actor, and businessman. His music often portrays an island escapism lifestyle. Buffett has a devoted fan base known as Parrot Heads.

Chopra, Deepak (b. 1946)

Chopra is an Indian-born American author. A prominent figure in the New Age movement, Chopra's books and videos have made him one of the best known and wealthiest figures in alternative medicine.

Cohen, Randy (b. 1948)

Cohen is an American writer and humorist renowned as the author of "The Ethicist," a column in the *New York Times Magazine* from 1999–2011. Cohen has authored several books and plays and is the host of the public radio show *Person Place Thing*.

Connors, Neila (b. 1953)

Dr. Neila Conners is the founder and president of Networking and Client (NAC) Connections, Inc. Her corporation is dedicated to the implementation of positive attitudes and actions in people.

Deford, Frank (1938–2017)

Deford was an American sportswriter and novelist. He wrote for *Sports Illustrated* from 1962 until his death in 2017. Deford was voted National Sportswriter of the Year six times by the members of that organization, and he was twice voted Magazine Writer of the Year by the *Washington Journalism Review.*

DuFour, Richard (1947–2017)

DuFour was an American educational researcher noted for developing strategies to create collaborative teaching environments in K-12 schools. Among other works, DuFour authored *Professional Learning Communities at Work* in 1998.

Durkheim, Emile (1858–1917)

Durkheim was a French sociologist whose work and editorship of the first journal of sociology helped establish sociology as an accepted social science. As a result, Durkheim is often referred to as "The Father of Sociology."

Eiseley, Loren (1907–1977)

Eiseley was an American anthropologist, educator, philosopher, and natural science writer. His most notable books include *The Immense Journey* (1957), *Darwin's Century* (1958), and *The Unexpected Universe* (1969). His story "The Star Thrower" is included in *The Unexpected Universe.*

Eliot, T. S. (1888–1965)

Thomas Stearns Eliot was a poet, essayist, playwright, and literary critic. Considered one of the twentieth century's major poets, Eliot was awarded the Nobel Prize in Literature in 1948.

Fitzgerald, Zelda (1900–1948)

Fitzgerald was an American socialite, novelist, and painter. Noted for her beauty and high spirits, Fitzgerald was dubbed "the first American flapper" by her husband, F. Scott.

Gardner, John W. (1912–2002)

Gardner was the United States Secretary of Health, Education, and Welfare from 1965–1968. He was a strong advocate for citizen participation and founded Common Cause.

Goethe, Johann Wolfgang von (1749–1832)

Goethe was a German poet, playwright, novelist, scientist, and statesman. He is considered to be the greatest German literary figure of the modern era.

Haley, Alex (1921–1992)

Haley was an American writer and the author of the 1976 book *Roots: The Saga of an American Family*. In 1977, ABC adapted *Roots* and created a television miniseries. The book and the miniseries raised the public's awareness of Black American history.

Hubbard, Elbert (1856–1915)

Hubbard was an American writer, publisher, artist, and philosopher. Best known as the founder of the Roycroft artisan community in East Aurora, N.Y., Hubbard was an influential member of the Arts and Crafts movement.

Humes, James (1934–2020)

Humes was an author and former presidential speechwriter. Along with William Safire and Pat Buchanan, Humes wrote the text on the Apollo 11 lunar plaque: "Here men from the planet Earth first set foot upon the Moon July 1969, A.D. We came in peace for all mankind."

Iacocca, Lee (1924–2019)

Iacocca was an automobile executive best known for his development of the Ford Mustang and the Ford Pinto. He was president and CEO of Chrysler from 1978 and chairman from 1979 until his retirement in 1992.

Jefferson, Thomas (1743–1826)

Jefferson was an American statesman, diplomat, lawyer, architect, and philosopher. One of the Founding Fathers, Jefferson served as the third president of the United States from 1801–1809.

Jung, Carl (1875–1961)

Jung was a Swiss psychiatrist and psychoanalyst who founded analytical psychology. Jung authored many books and articles including *Psychology of the Unconscious* (1912), *Modern Man in Search of a Soul* (1933), and *Answer to Job* (1952).

Keohane, Nannerl (b. 1940)

Dr. Keohane is an American political theorist and the former president of both Wellesley College and Duke University. Keohane continues to teach in renowned settings such as Princeton University and Oxford.

King, Martin Luther, Jr. (1929–1968)

Martin Luther King, Jr., was an American Baptist minister and activist who became the most visible spokesman and leader in the Civil Rights Movement from 1955 until his assassination in 1968.

Lamott, Anne (b. 1954)

Lamott is a progressive political activist, public speaker, and writing teacher. Her nonfiction books, which are largely autobiographical, include *Bird by Bird* (1994), *Traveling Mercies* (1999), and *Grace (Eventually)* (2007).

Lombardi, Vince (1913–1970)

Lombardi was an American football coach and executive in the National Football League. He is best known as the head coach of the Green Bay Packers during the 1960s.

Longfellow, Henry Wadsworth (1807–1882)

An American poet and educator, Longfellow was one of the fireside poets from New England. He wrote many lyric poems known for their musicality and often presenting stories of mythology and legend. Longfellow became the most popular poet of his day.

Machiavelli, Niccolò (1469–1527)

Machiavelli was an Italian diplomat, author, philosopher, and historian who lived during the Renaissance. He has often been called "the father of modern political science." Machiavelli's best-known political treatise is *The Prince* (1513).

McDonnell, Sanford (1922–2012)

McDonnell was an American engineer, businessman, and philanthropist. He was the former chairman and chief executive officer of McDonnell Douglas Corp.

Model of Concentric Circles (2012)

The Model of Concentric Circles was envisioned and described by Dennis F. Herrick in *Media Management in the Age of Giants: Business Dynamics of Journalism* (2012).

Molière (1622–1673)

Molière was a French playwright, actor, and poet. Born Jean-Baptiste Poquelin, he took "Molière" as his stage name. He is widely regarded as one of the greatest French-language writers in world literature.

O'Donnell, Jim (b. 1973)

O'Donnell is a writer, photographer, and explorer based in Taos, New Mexico. An extreme traveler, O'Donnell categorizes his blogs by the countries that informed or inspired his thoughts.

Paige, Satchel (1906–1982)

Paige was an American professional baseball player who played in Negro League Baseball and Major League Baseball. His career spanned five decades and culminated with his induction into the National Baseball Hall of Fame.

Quick, Matthew (b. 1973)

Quick is an American writer of adult and young adult fiction. His debut novel, *The Silver Linings Playbook*, became a *New York Times* bestseller and was adapted as a movie of the same name.

Quindlen, Anna (b. 1953)

Quindlen is an American author, journalist, and opinion columnist. Her works of nonfiction include *Living Out Loud* (1988), *A Short Guide to a Happy Life* (2000), *Loud and Clear* (2004), and *Lots of Candles, Plenty of Cake* (2012).

Radmacher, Mary Anne (b. 1957)

Radmacher is an American writer and artist. She conducts workshops on living a full, creative, balanced life. Writing since she was a child, Radmacher uses her writing to explore symbols and find meaning.

Remnick, David (b. 1958)

Remnick has been editor of *The New Yorker* since 1998 and a staff writer since 1992. The American journalist won a Pulitzer Prize in 1994 for his book *Lenin's Tomb*.

Robinson, Edwin Arlington (1869–1935)

An American poet, Robinson won a Pulitzer Prize for Poetry on three occasions and was nominated for the Nobel Prize in Literature four times.

Schweitzer, Albert (1875–1965)

Schweitzer was a German theologian, writer, philosopher, and physician. He won the Nobel Peace Prize in 1952 for his philosophy of "Reverence for Life."

Sergiovanni, Thomas (1937–2012)

A professor at Trinity University in San Antonio, Texas, Sergiovanni advocated for ideas-based leadership. He believed in community responsibility where leadership is shared. Sergiovanni's ideas are practical models of leadership, which acknowledge the messy world of education.

Shaw, George Bernard (1856–1950)

Shaw was an Irish playwright, critic, and political activist. His influence on Western theatre was profound. Shaw wrote sixty plays, including *Man and Superman* (1902) and *Pygmalion* (1912).

Stone, Elizabeth (b. 1946)

Stone is a professor of English at Fordham University in New York. Her research and teaching interests include creative nonfiction, twentieth-century American autobiography, and memoir.

Teilhard de Chardin, Pierre (1881–1955)

Teilhard de Chardin was a French Jesuit priest, theologian, philosopher, and teacher. Darwinian in outlook, Teilhard de Chardin authored several influential theological and philosophical books.

Thatcher, Margaret (1925–2013)

Thatcher was Prime Minister of the United Kingdom from 1979–1990. A Soviet journalist dubbed her the "Iron Lady," a nickname that became associated with her uncompromising politics and leadership style.

"Tin Man" (1974)

The pop rock band America produced the song "Tin Man" in 1974. The hit tune was written by band member Dewey Bunnell.

Twain, Mark (1835–1910)

Born Samuel Langhorne Clemens, Twain was an American writer, humorist, entrepreneur, and lecturer. He was lauded as the greatest humorist the United States has produced. William Faulkner called Twain "the father of American literature."

Wheatley, Margaret (b. 1944)

Wheatley is an American writer, teacher, speaker, and management consultant who works to create organizations and communities worthy of human habitation. Among her published books are *A Simpler Way* (1996), *Turning to One Another* (2002), *Finding Our Way: Leadership for an Uncertain Time* (2005), and *Who Do We Choose to Be?* (2017).

Wingate, Lisa (b. 1965)

Wingate is an American inspirational speaker and the author of thirty novels. Her debut novel was *Tending Roses* (2001), and in 2017, she published *Before We Were Yours*, which remained on the *New York Times* bestseller list for fifty-four weeks.

Zander, Benjamin (b. 1939); Zander, Rosamund Stone (b. 1942)

The Art of Possibility (2000) was co-authored by the Zanders and blends lessons Rosamund learned from her work as a family therapist and executive coach with Benjamin's leadership practices as the director and cofounder of the Boston Philharmonic Orchestra.

Acknowledgments

Lessons That Endure has been a long time in the making. I am grateful for the legions of family members and friends who patiently endured my telling (and retelling) of stories about my work. Your responses to those tales helped me to select the lessons that resonated most clearly and broadly.

I am grateful to the Parkway School District for the incredible opportunities to grow professionally and, at the same time, discover and embrace lifelong friends.

Many thanks to the Fern Ridge High School and Parkway West High School teachers, students, staff, and parents whom I was privileged to serve for so many years. You held me up on the good days and struggled with me through the rough ones. In the process, we learned what true community looks like.

When asked, my former Mustang and Longhorn colleagues dug through their school files to help their former boss find artifacts, information, and pictures to help my reflections come to life more vividly. I miss the joy and ease of working with you.

Once my thoughts were finally in readable form, I am grateful to the colleagues and friends who graciously read the manuscript and provided thoughtful feedback: Michael Barolak, Jim Brecker, Nancy Giulvezan, Jere Hochman, Nan Johnson, Jenny Marquart, Doug Thaman, and Rebecca Warren.

My support team at Davis Creative Publishing were knowledgeable and patient and deserve extensive credit. Without their help and guidance, this rookie author would not have a book in her hand.

My children, their wives, and my extraordinary grandchildren offered practical supports and creative advice for which I am most grateful. But being a "bad-ass grandma" for writing a book may be the highest praise of all.

And then there is Becky Warren. When I had literally stuffed the manuscript into a drawer and simply quit, my dear friend said, "Not so fast." Becky became my most relentless critic, advocate, and, in the end, the catalyst that birthed this book. I am forever grateful.

Printed in Great Britain
by Amazon

33373898R00106